MznLnx

Missing Links Exam Preps

Exam Prep for

Management : A Practical Introduction

Kinicki & Williams, 4th Edition

The MznLnx Exam Prep is your link from the texbook and lecture to your exams.
The MznLnx Exam Preps are unauthorized and comprehensive reviews of your textbooks.

All material provided by MznLnx and Rico Publications (c) 2010
Textbook publishers and textbook authors do not particpate in or contribute to these reviews.

MznLnx

Rico
Publications

Exam Prep for Management : A Practical Introduction
4th Edition
Kinicki & Williams

Publisher: Raymond Houge
Assistant Editor: Michael Rouger
Text and Cover Designer: Lisa Buckner
Marketing Manager: Sara Swagger
Project Manager, Editorial Production: Jerry Emerson
Art Director: Vernon Lowerui

Product Manager: Dave Mason
Editorial Assitant: Rachel Guzmanji
Pedagogy: Debra Long
Cover Image: Jim Reed/Getty Images
Text and Cover Printer: City Printing, Inc.
Compositor: Media Mix, Inc.

(c) 2010 Rico Publications
ALL RIGHTS RESERVED. No part of this work
covered by the copyright may be reproduced or
used in any form or by an means--graphic, electronic,
or mechanical, including photocopying, recording,
taping, Web distribution, information storage, and
retrieval systems, or in any other manner--without the
written permission of the publisher.

Printed in the United States
ISBN:

For more information about our products, contact us at:
Dave.Mason@RicoPublications.com

For permission to use material from this text or
product, submit a request online to:
Dave.Mason@RicoPublications.com

Contents

CHAPTER 1
The Exceptional Manager: What You Do, How You Do It — 1

CHAPTER 2
Management Theory: Essential Background for the Successful Manager — 13

CHAPTER 3
The Manager's Changing Work Environment & Ethical Responsibilities — 22

CHAPTER 4
Global Management: Managing across Borders — 34

CHAPTER 5
Planning: The Foundation of Successful Management — 45

CHAPTER 6
Strategic Management: How Star Managers Realize a Grand Design — 52

CHAPTER 7
Individual & Group Decision Making: How Managers Make Things Happen — 64

CHAPTER 8
Organizational Culture, Structure, & Design — 72

CHAPTER 9
Human Resource Management: Getting the Right People for Managerial Success — 79

CHAPTER 10
Organizational Change & Innovation — 92

CHAPTER 11
Managing Individual Differences & Behavior: Supervising People as People — 100

CHAPTER 12
Motivating Employees: Achieving Superior Performance in the Workplace — 107

CHAPTER 13
Groups & Teams: Increasing Cooperation, Reducing Conflict — 117

CHAPTER 14
Power, Influence, & Leadership: From Becoming a Manager to Becoming a Leader — 123

CHAPTER 15
Interpersonal & Organizational Communication — 128

CHAPTER 16
Control: Techniques for Enhancing Organizational Effectiveness — 133

ANSWER KEY — 150

TO THE STUDENT

COMPREHENSIVE

The *MznLnx* Exam Prep series is designed to help you pass your exams. Editors at MznLnx review your textbooks and then prepare these practice exams to help you master the textbook material. Unlike study guides, workbooks, and practice tests provided by the texbook publisher and textbook authors, *MznLnx* gives you **all** of the material in each chapter in exam form, not just samples, so you can be sure to nail your exam.

MECHANICAL

The MznLnx Exam Prep series creates exams that will help you learn the subject matter as well as test you on your understanding. Each question is designed to help you master the concept. Just working through the exams, you gain an understanding of the subject--its a simple mechanical process that produces success.

INTEGRATED STUDY GUIDE AND REVIEW

MznLnx is not just a set of exams designed to test you, its also a comprehensive review of the subject content. Each exam question is also a review of the concept, making sure that you will get the answer correct without having to go to other sources of material. You learn as you go! Its the easiest way to pass an exam.

HUMOR

Studying can be tedious and dry. MznLnx's instructional design includes moderate humor within the exam questions on occassion, to break the tedium and revitalize the brain

Chapter 1. The Exceptional Manager: What You Do, How You Do It 1

1. _____ has been described as the 'process of social influence in which one person can enlist the aid and support of others in the accomplishment of a common task' . A definition more inclusive of followers comes from Alan Keith of Genentech who said '_____ is ultimately about creating a way for people to contribute to making something extraordinary happen.'

_____ is one of the most salient aspects of the organizational context. However, defining _____ has been challenging.

   a. Leadership
   b. Situational leadership
   c. 1990 Clean Air Act
   d. 28-hour day

2. The _____ (Situation, Task, Action, Result) format is a job interview technique used by interviewers to gather all the relevant information about a specific capability that the job requires. This interview format is said to have a higher degree of predictability of future on-the-job performance than the traditional interview.

   - Situation: The interviewer wants you to present a recent challenge and situation in which you found yourself.
   - Task: What did you have to achieve? The interviewer will be looking to see what you were trying to achieve from the situation.
   - Action: What did you do? The interviewer will be looking for information on what you did, why you did it and what were the alternatives.
   - Results: What was the outcome of your actions? What did you achieve through your actions and did you meet your objectives. What did you learn from this experience and have you used this learning since?

   a. Rasch models
   b. Phrase completion
   c. Competency-based job descriptions
   d. Star

3. _____ is one of the managerial functions like planning, organizing, staffing and directing. It is an important function because it helps to check the errors and to take the corrective action so that deviation from standards are minimized and stated goals of the organization are achieved in desired manner.According to modern concepts, _____ is a foreseeing action whereas earlier concept of _____ was used only when errors were detected. _____ in management means setting standards, measuring actual performance and taking corrective action.

   a. Turnover
   b. Control
   c. Schedule of reinforcement
   d. Decision tree pruning

4. A _____ is a process in which a potential employee is evaluated by an employer for prospective employment in their company, organization and was established in the late 16th century.

A _____ typically precedes the hiring decision, and is used to evaluate the candidate. The interview is usually preceded by the evaluation of submitted résumés from interested candidates, then selecting a small number of candidates for interviews.

   a. Payrolling
   b. Supported employment
   c. Split shift
   d. Job interview

5. A _____ or chief executive is one of the highest-ranking corporate officer (executive) or administrator in charge of total management. An individual selected as President and _____ of a corporation, company, organization, or agency, reports to the board of directors. In internal communication and press releases, many companies capitalize the term and those of other high positions, even when they are not proper nouns.
   - a. Financial analyst
   - b. Chief executive officer
   - c. Chief brand officer
   - d. Purchasing manager

6. In economics and sociology, an _____ is any factor (financial or non-financial) that enables or motivates a particular course of action, or counts as a reason for preferring one choice to the alternatives. It is an expectation that encourages people to behave in a certain way. Since human beings are purposeful creatures, the study of _____ structures is central to the study of all economic activity (both in terms of individual decision-making and in terms of co-operation and competition within a larger institutional structure.)
   - a. Incentive
   - b. AAAI
   - c. A Stake in the Outcome
   - d. A4e

7. While _____ literally refers to a person responsible for the performance of duties involved in running an organization, the exact meaning of the role is variable, depending on the organization.

While there is no clear line between executive or principal and inferior officers, principal officers are high-level officials in the executive branch of U.S. government such as department heads of independent agencies. In Humphrey's Executor v. United States, 295 U.S. 602 (1935), the Court distinguished between _____s and quasi-legislative or quasi-judicial officers by stating that the former serve at the pleasure of the President and may be removed at his discretion.

   - a. Executive officer
   - b. Unreported employment
   - c. Australian Fair Pay and Conditions Standard
   - d. Easement

8. _____ in its literal sense is the process of transformation of local or regional phenomena into global ones. It can be described as a process by which the people of the world are unified into a single society and function together.

This process is a combination of economic, technological, sociocultural and political forces.

   - a. Histogram
   - b. Collaborative Planning, Forecasting and Replenishment
   - c. Globalization
   - d. Cost Management

9. _____ is, in very basic words, a position a firm occupies against its competitors.

According to Michael Porter, the three methods for creating a sustainable _____ are through:

1. Cost leadership

2. Differentiation

3. Focus (economics)

a. 1990 Clean Air Act
b. 28-hour day
c. Competitive advantage
d. Theory Z

10. _____ is the provision of service to customers before, during and after a purchase.

According to Turban et al. (2002), '_____ is a series of activities designed to enhance the level of customer satisfaction - that is, the feeling that a product or service has met the customer expectation.'

Its importance varies by product, industry and customer; defective or broken merchandise can be exchanged, often only with a receipt and within a specified time frame.

a. 28-hour day
b. 1990 Clean Air Act
c. Service rate
d. Customer service

11. _____ refers to metrics and measures of output from production processes, per unit of input. Labor _____, for example, is typically measured as a ratio of output per labor-hour, an input. _____ may be conceived of as a metrics of the technical or engineering efficiency of production.

a. Value engineering
b. Remanufacturing
c. Master production schedule
d. Productivity

12. _____ is an advertisement in which a particular product specifically mentions a competitor by name for the express purpose of showing why the competitor is inferior to the product naming it.

This should not be confused with parody advertisements, where a fictional product is being advertised for the purpose of poking fun at the particular advertisement, nor should it be confused with the use of a coined brand name for the purpose of comparing the product without actually naming an actual competitor. ('Wikipedia tastes better and is less filling than the Encyclopedia Galactica.')

In the 1980s, during what has been referred to as the cola wars, soft-drink manufacturer Pepsi ran a series of advertisements where people, caught on hidden camera, in a blind taste test, chose Pepsi over rival Coca-Cola.

a. Comparative advertising
b. 33 Strategies of War
c. 28-hour day
d. 1990 Clean Air Act

13. _____ is a form of communication that typically attempts to persuade potential customers to purchase or to consume more of a particular brand of product or service. 'While now central to the contemporary global economy and the reproduction of global production networks, it is only quite recently that _____ has been more than a marginal influence on patterns of sales and production. The formation of modern _____ was intimately bound up with the emergence of new forms of monopoly capitalism around the end of the 19th and beginning of the 20th century as one element in corporate strategies to create, organize and where possible control markets, especially for mass produced consumer goods.

a. AAAI
b. A Stake in the Outcome
c. A4e
d. Advertising

14. A _____ is a name or trademark connected with a product or producer. _____s have become increasingly important components of culture and the economy, now being described as 'cultural accessories and personal philosophies'.

Some people distinguish the psychological aspect of a _____ from the experiential aspect.

a. Brand awareness
b. Brand extension
c. Brand loyalty
d. Brand

15. The 'business case for _____', theorizes that in a global marketplace, a company that employs a diverse workforce (both men and women, people of many generations, people from ethnically and racially diverse backgrounds etc.) is better able to understand the demographics of the marketplace it serves and is thus better equipped to thrive in that marketplace than a company that has a more limited range of employee demographics.

An additional corollary suggests that a company that supports the _____ of its workforce can also improve employee satisfaction, productivity and retention.

a. Trademark
b. Virtual team
c. Kanban
d. Diversity

16. _____ is an idea in the field of Organizational studies and management which describes the psychology, attitudes, experiences, beliefs and Values (personal and cultural values) of an organization. It has been defined as 'the specific collection of values and norms that are shared by people and groups in an organization and that control the way they interact with each other and with stakeholders outside the organization.'

This definition continues to explain organizational values also known as 'beliefs and ideas about what kinds of goals members of an organization should pursue and ideas about the appropriate kinds or standards of behavior organizational members should use to achieve these goals. From organizational values develop organizational norms, guidelines or expectations that prescribe appropriate kinds of behavior by employees in particular situations and control the behavior of organizational members towards one another.'

_____ is not the same as corporate culture.

a. Organizational development
b. Organizational culture
c. Organizational effectiveness
d. Union shop

17. _____ can be regarded as an outcome of mental processes (cognitive process) leading to the selection of a course of action among several alternatives. Every _____ process produces a final choice. The output can be an action or an opinion of choice.

a. 1990 Clean Air Act
b. 28-hour day
c. 33 Strategies of War
d. Decision making

18. _____, commonly referred to as 'eBusiness' or 'e-Business', may be defined as the utilization of information and communication technologies (ICT) in support of all the activities of business. Commerce constitutes the exchange of products and services between businesses, groups and individuals and hence can be seen as one of the essential activities of any business. Hence, electronic commerce or eCommerce focuses on the use of ICT to enable the external activities and relationships of the business with individuals, groups and other businesses.

a. AAAI
b. A4e
c. A Stake in the Outcome
d. Electronic business

19. _____, commonly known as e-commerce, consists of the buying and selling of products or services over electronic systems such as the Internet and other computer networks. The amount of trade conducted electronically has grown extraordinarily with widespread Internet usage. The use of commerce is conducted in this way, spurring and drawing on innovations in electronic funds transfer, supply chain management, Internet marketing, online transaction processing, electronic data interchange (EDI), inventory management systems, and automated data collection systems.

a. Online shopping
b. Electronic Commerce
c. A4e
d. A Stake in the Outcome

20. _____ comprises a range of practices used in an organisation to identify, create, represent, distribute and enable adoption of insights and experiences. Such insights and experiences comprise knowledge, either embodied in individuals or embedded in organisational processes or practice.

An established discipline since 1991 , _____ includes courses taught in the fields of business administration, information systems, management, and library and information sciences .

a. 28-hour day
b. 33 Strategies of War
c. 1990 Clean Air Act
d. Knowledge management

21. An _____ is a mostly hierarchical concept of subordination of entities that collaborate and contribute to serve one common aim.

Organizations are a variant of clustered entities. The structure of an organization is usually set up in many a styles, dependent on their objectives and ambience.

a. Organizational development
b. Organizational structure
c. Open shop
d. Informal organization

22. _____ is subcontracting a process, such as product design or manufacturing, to a third-party company. The decision to outsource is often made in the interest of lowering cost or making better use of time and energy costs, redirecting or conserving energy directed at the competencies of a particular business, or to make more efficient use of land, labor, capital, (information) technology and resources. _____ became part of the business lexicon during the 1980s.

a. Outsourcing
b. Unemployment insurance
c. Operant conditioning
d. Opinion leadership

23. _____ refers to the movement of cash into or out of a business or financial product. It is usually measured during a specified, finite period of time. Measurement of _____ can be used

- to determine a project's rate of return or value. The time of _____s into and out of projects are used as inputs in financial models such as internal rate of return, and net present value.
- to determine problems with a business's liquidity. Being profitable does not necessarily mean being liquid. A company can fail because of a shortage of cash, even while profitable.
- as an alternate measure of a business's profits when it is believed that accrual accounting concepts do not represent economic realities. For example, a company may be notionally profitable but generating little operational cash (as may be the case for a company that barters its products rather than selling for cash.) In such a case, the company may be deriving additional operating cash by issuing shares evaluating default risk, re-investment requirements, etc.

_____ is a generic term used differently depending on the context. It may be defined by users for their own purposes.

a. Gross profit
b. Sweat equity
c. Cash flow
d. Gross profit margin

24. _____ is the discipline of planning, organizing and managing resources to bring about the successful completion of specific project goals and objectives. It is often closely related to and sometimes conflated with Program management.

A project is a finite endeavor--having specific start and completion dates--undertaken to meet particular goals and objectives, usually to bring about beneficial change or added value.

a. Project engineer
b. Work package
c. Project management
d. Precedence diagram

25. _____, e-commuting, e-work, telework, working from home (WFH), or working at home (WAH) is a work arrangement in which employees enjoy flexibility in working location and hours. In other words, the daily commute to a central place of work is replaced by telecommunication links. Many work from home, while others, occasionally also referred to as nomad workers or web commuters utilize mobile telecommunications technology to work from coffee shops or myriad other locations.

a. Telecommuting
b. 28-hour day
c. 1990 Clean Air Act
d. 33 Strategies of War

26. A _____ -- also known as a geographically dispersed team -- is a group of individuals who work across time, space, and organizational boundaries with links strengthened by webs of communication technology. They have complementary skills and are committed to a common purpose, have interdependent performance goals, and share an approach to work for which they hold themselves mutually accountable. Geographically dispersed teams allow organizations to hire and retain the best people regardless of location.

a. Trademark
b. Kanban
c. Risk management
d. Virtual team

27. _____ is a concept related to the relative abilities of parties in a situation to exert influence over each other. If both parties are on an equal footing in a debate, then they will have equal _____, such as in a perfectly competitive market, or between an evenly matched monopoly and monopsony.

There are a number of fields where the concept of _____ has proven crucial to coherent analysis: game theory, labour economics, collective bargaining arrangements, diplomatic negotiations, settlement of litigation, the price of insurance, and any negotiation in general.

- a. 1990 Clean Air Act
- b. Buy-sell agreement
- c. Bargaining power
- d. Trade credit

28. _____ involves establishing specific, measurable and time-targeted objectives. Work on the theory of goal-setting suggests that it's an effective tool for making progress by ensuring that participants in a group with a common goal are clearly aware of what is expected from them if an objective is to be achieved. On a personal level, setting goals is a process that allows people to specify then work towards their own objectives - most commonly with financial or career-based goals.

- a. Resource-based view
- b. Digital strategy
- c. Catfish effect
- d. Goal setting

29. In economics, a _____ exists when a specific individual or enterprise has sufficient control over a particular product or service to determine significantly the terms on which other individuals shall have access to it. Monopolies are thus characterized by a lack of economic competition for the good or service that they provide and a lack of viable substitute goods. The verb 'monopolize' refers to the process by which a firm gains persistently greater market share than what is expected under perfect competition.

- a. 33 Strategies of War
- b. Monopoly
- c. 1990 Clean Air Act
- d. 28-hour day

30. _____ is a process of planning and controlling the performance or execution of any type of activity, such as:

- a project (project _____) or
- a process (process _____, sometimes referred to as the process performance measurement and management system.)

Organization's senior management is responsible for carrying out its _____.

- a. Participatory management
- b. Human Relations Movement
- c. Work design
- d. Management process

31. _____ is an organization's process of defining its strategy and making decisions on allocating its resources to pursue this strategy, including its capital and people. Various business analysis techniques can be used in _____, including SWOT analysis (Strengths, Weaknesses, Opportunities, and Threats) and PEST analysis (Political, Economic, Social, and Technological analysis) or STEER analysis involving Socio-cultural, Technological, Economic, Ecological, and Regulatory factors and EPISTEL (Environment, Political, Informatic, Social, Technological, Economic and Legal)

_____ is the formal consideration of an organization's future course. All _____ deals with at least one of three key questions:

1. 'What do we do?'
2. 'For whom do we do it?'
3. 'How do we excel?'

In business _____, the third question is better phrased 'How can we beat or avoid competition?'. (Bradford and Duncan, page 1.)

a. Strategic planning
b. 33 Strategies of War
c. 28-hour day
d. 1990 Clean Air Act

32. A _____ is a list of the general tasks and responsibilities of a position. Typically, it also includes to whom the position reports, specifications such as the qualifications needed by the person in the job, salary range for the position, etc. A _____ is usually developed by conducting a job analysis, which includes examining the tasks and sequences of tasks necessary to perform the job.

a. Recruitment
b. Recruitment Process Insourcing
c. Recruitment advertising
d. Job description

33. A _____ in today's workforce is an individual that is valued for their ability to interpret information within a specific subject area. They will often advance the overall understanding of that subject through focused analysis, design and/or development. They use research skills to define problems and to identify alternatives.

a. Career development
b. Customer satisfaction
c. Knowledge worker
d. Business rule

34. _____ for short is a descriptive term for certain executives in a business operation. It is also a formal title held by some business executives, most commonly in the hospitality industry.

A _____ has broad, overall responsibility for a business or organization. Whereas a manager may be responsible for one functional area, the _____ is responsible for all areas.

a. Chief knowledge officer
b. General manager
c. Chief technology officer
d. Managing director

35. _____ is a term defined by the Oxford English Dictionary as an individual's 'course or progress through life '. It is usually considered to pertain to remunerative work (and sometimes also formal education.)

The etymology of the term is somewhat ironic in that it comes from the Latin word carrera, which means race .

a. Career
b. Spatial mismatch
c. Career planning
d. Nursing shortage

36. In politics, a _____, (by metaphor with the carved _____ at the prow of a sailing ship), is a person who holds an important title or office yet executes little actual power, most commonly limited by convention rather than law. Common _____s include constitutional monarchs, such as: Queen Elizabeth II, the Emperor of Japan, or presidents in parliamentary democracies, such as the President of Israel.

While the authority of a _____ is in practice generally symbolic, public opinion, respect for the office or the office holder and access to high levels of government can give them significant influence on events.

   a. Figurehead
   c. 1990 Clean Air Act
   b. 33 Strategies of War
   d. 28-hour day

37. _____ refers to a range of skills, tools, and techniques used to manage time when accomplishing specific tasks, projects and goals. This set encompass a wide scope of activities, and these include planning, allocating, setting goals, delegation, analysis of time spent, monitoring, organizing, scheduling, and prioritizing. Initially _____ referred to just business or work activities, but eventually the term broadened to include personal activities also.
   a. Cash cow
   c. Voice of the customer
   b. Time management
   d. Formula for Change

38. An _____ is a person who has possession of an enterprise and assumes significant accountability for the inherent risks and the outcome. It is an ambitious leader who combines land, labor, and capital to create and market new goods or services. The term is a loanword from French and was first defined by the Irish economist Richard Cantillon.
   a. Entrepreneur
   c. A Stake in the Outcome
   b. AAAI
   d. A4e

39. _____ according to Onuoha (2007) is the practice of starting new organizations or revitalizing mature organizations, particularly new businesses generally in response to identified opportunities. _____ is often a difficult undertaking, as a vast majority of new businesses fail. Entrepreneurial activities are substantially different depending on the type of organization that is being started.
   a. Entrepreneurship
   c. AAAI
   b. A Stake in the Outcome
   d. A4e

40. In decision theory and estimation theory, the _____ of an estimator, $\hat{\theta}$, of an unknown parameter of the distribution, θ, is the expected value of the loss function

$$R(\theta, \hat{\theta}) = \mathbb{E}_\theta L(\theta, \hat{\theta}) = \int L(\theta, \hat{\theta})\, dP_\theta.$$

where dP_θ is a probability measure parametrized by θ.

- For a scalar parameter θ and a quadratic loss function,

$$L(\theta, \hat{\theta}) = (\theta - \hat{\theta})^2$$

the _____ function becomes the mean squared error of the estimate,

$$R(\theta, \hat{\theta}) = E_\theta(\theta - \hat{\theta})^2$$

- In density estimation, the unknown parameter is probability density itself. The loss function is typically chosen to be a norm in an appropriate function space. For example, for L^2 norm,

$$L(f, \hat{f}) = \|f - \hat{f}\|_2^2$$

the _____ function becomes the mean integrated squared error

$$R(f, \hat{f}) = E\|f - \hat{f}\|^2$$

a. Financial modeling
c. Linear model
b. Risk aversion
d. Risk

41. _____ is a term in psychology which refers to a person's belief about what causes the good or bad results in his or her life, either in general or in a specific area such as health or academics. Understanding of the concept was developed by Julian B. Rotter in 1954, and has since become an important aspect of personality studies.

_____ refers to the extent to which individuals believe that they can control events that affect them.

a. Machiavellianism
c. Locus of control
b. Social loafing
d. Self-enhancement

42. _____ refers to an individual's desire for significant accomplishment, mastering of skills, control, or high standards. The term was introduced by the psychologist, David McClelland.

_____ is related to the difficulty of tasks people choose to undertake.

a. Need for achievement
c. Need for power
b. Two-factor theory
d. 1990 Clean Air Act

43. The inverse of a person's risk aversion is sometimes called their _____

A person is given the choice between two scenarios, one with a guaranteed payoff and one without. In the guaranteed scenario, the person receives $50. In the uncertain scenario, a coin is flipped to decide whether the person receives $100 or nothing. The expected payoff for both scenarios is $50, meaning that an individual who was insensitive to risk would not care whether they took the guaranteed payment or the gamble.

a. Discounting
b. Risk tolerance
c. Risk
d. Ruin theory

44. Engineering _____ is the permissible limit of variation in

   1. a physical dimension,
   2. a measured value or physical property of a material, manufactured object, system, or service,
   3. other measured values (such as temperature, humidity, etc.)
   4. in engineering and safety, a physical distance or space (_____), as in a truck (lorry), train or boat under a bridge as well as a train in a tunnel

Dimensions, properties, or conditions may vary within certain practical limits without significantly affecting functioning of equipment or a process. _____s are specified to allow reasonable leeway for imperfections and inherent variability without compromising performance.

The _____ may be specified as a factor or percentage of the nominal value, a maximum deviation from a nominal value, an explicit range of allowed values, be specified by a note or published standard with this information, or be implied by the numeric accuracy of the nominal value. _____ can be symmetrical, as in 40±0.1, or asymmetrical, such as 40+0.2/−0.1.

a. Zero defects
b. Quality assurance
c. Tolerance
d. Root cause analysis

45. '_____' refers to mental and communicative algorithms applied during social communications and interactions in order to reach certain effects or results. The term '_____' is used often in business contexts to refer to the measure of a person's ability to operate within business organizations through social communication and interactions. _____ are how people relate to one another.

a. AAAI
b. A4e
c. A Stake in the Outcome
d. Interpersonal skills

46. The _____ captures an expanded spectrum of values and criteria for measuring organizational success: economic, ecological and social. With the ratification of the United Nations and ICLEI _____ standard for urban and community accounting in early 2007, this became the dominant approach to public sector full cost accounting. Similar UN standards apply to natural capital and human capital measurement to assist in measurements required by _____, e.g. the ecoBudget standard for reporting ecological footprint.

a. Triple bottom line
b. 28-hour day
c. 1990 Clean Air Act
d. 33 Strategies of War

47. _____ is a pedagogical concept according to which newly acquired skills should be practiced well beyond the point of initial mastery, leading to automaticity.

The Yerkes-Dodson law predicts that _____ can improve performance in states of high arousal.

a. A Stake in the Outcome
b. A4e
c. AAAI
d. Overlearning

Chapter 2. Management Theory: Essential Background for the Successful Manager

1. _____ is an emerging movement to explicitly use the current, best evidence in management decision-making. Its roots are in evidence-based medicine, a quality movement to apply the scientific method to medical practice.

_____ entails managerial decisions and organizational practices informed by the best available scientific evidence.

- a. Anti-leadership
- b. Entrenchment Management
- c. Enterprise Decision Management
- d. Evidence-based management

2. _____ refers to bodies of techniques for investigating phenomena, acquiring new knowledge, or correcting and integrating previous knowledge. To be termed scientific, a method of inquiry must be based on gathering observable, empirical and measurable evidence subject to specific principles of reasoning. A _____ consists of the collection of data through observation and experimentation, and the formulation and testing of hypotheses.
- a. 28-hour day
- b. 1990 Clean Air Act
- c. 33 Strategies of War
- d. Scientific method

3. The term '_____' refers to the concept of collecting information and attempting to spot a pattern in the information. In some fields of study, the term '_____' has more formally-defined meanings.

In project management _____ is a mathematical technique that uses historical results to predict future outcome.

- a. Regression analysis
- b. Least squares
- c. Trend analysis
- d. Stepwise regression

4. A _____ is the term given to a company that facilitates the learning of its members and continuously transforms itself. _____s develop as a result of the pressures facing modern organizations and enables them to remain competitive in the business environment. A _____ has five main features; systems thinking, personal mastery, mental models, shared vision and team learning.
- a. 1990 Clean Air Act
- b. Hoshin Kanri
- c. Quality function deployment
- d. Learning organization

5. An _____ is a mostly hierarchical concept of subordination of entities that collaborate and contribute to serve one common aim.

Organizations are a variant of clustered entities. The structure of an organization is usually set up in many a styles, dependent on their objectives and ambience.

- a. Open shop
- b. Organizational structure
- c. Organizational development
- d. Informal organization

6. _____ is one of the managerial functions like planning, organizing, staffing and directing. It is an important function because it helps to check the errors and to take the corrective action so that deviation from standards are minimized and stated goals of the organization are achieved in desired manner. According to modern concepts, _____ is a foreseeing action whereas earlier concept of _____ was used only when errors were detected. _____ in management means setting standards, measuring actual performance and taking corrective action.

Chapter 2. Management Theory: Essential Background for the Successful Manager

  a. Control
  c. Decision tree pruning
  b. Schedule of reinforcement
  d. Turnover

7. _____ refers to metrics and measures of output from production processes, per unit of input. Labor _____, for example, is typically measured as a ratio of output per labor-hour, an input. _____ may be conceived of as a metrics of the technical or engineering efficiency of production.
  a. Master production schedule
  c. Remanufacturing
  b. Productivity
  d. Value engineering

8. _____ is a theory of management that analyzes and synthesizes workflows, with the objective of improving labour productivity. The core ideas of the theory were developed by Frederick Winslow Taylor in the 1880s and 1890s, and were first published in his monographs, Shop Management and The Principles of _____ Taylor believed that decisions based upon tradition and rules of thumb should be replaced by precise procedures developed after careful study of an individual at work.
  a. Master production schedule
  c. Capacity planning
  b. Value engineering
  d. Scientific management

9. In economics and sociology, an _____ is any factor (financial or non-financial) that enables or motivates a particular course of action, or counts as a reason for preferring one choice to the alternatives. It is an expectation that encourages people to behave in a certain way. Since human beings are purposeful creatures, the study of _____ structures is central to the study of all economic activity (both in terms of individual decision-making and in terms of co-operation and competition within a larger institutional structure.)
  a. A4e
  c. AAAI
  b. Incentive
  d. A Stake in the Outcome

10. A _____ is a compensation, usually financial, received by a worker in exchange for their labor.

Compensation in terms of _____s is given to worker and compensation in terms of salary is given to employees. Compensation is a monetary benefits given to employees in returns of the services provided by them.

  a. Profit-sharing agreement
  c. Performance-related pay
  b. State Compensation Insurance Fund
  d. Wage

11. _____ or Behaviourism thinking and feeling--can and should be regarded as behaviors. The school of psychology maintains that behaviors as such can be described scientifically without recourse either to internal physiological events or to hypothetical constructs such as the mind. _____ comprises the position that all theories should have observational correlates but that there are no philosophical differences between publicly observable processes and privately observable processes
  a. Borderline intellectual functioning
  c. Psychometrics
  b. Cognitive dissonance
  d. Behaviorism

12. The _____ is a form of reactivity whereby subjects improve an aspect of their behavior being experimentally measured simply in response to the fact that they are being studied, not in response to any particular experimental manipulation.

Chapter 2. Management Theory: Essential Background for the Successful Manager

The term was coined in 1955 by Henry A. Landsberger when analyzing older experiments from 1924-1932 at the Hawthorne Works (outside Chicago.) Hawthorne Works had commissioned a study to see if its workers would become more productive in higher or lower levels of light.

- a. 28-hour day
- b. Hawthorne effect
- c. 1990 Clean Air Act
- d. 33 Strategies of War

13. _____ Movement refers to those researchers of organizational development who study the behavior of people in groups, in particular workplace groups. It originated in the 1920s' Hawthorne studies, which examined the effects of social relations, motivation and employee satisfaction on factory productivity. The movement viewed workers in terms of their psychology and fit with companies, rather than as interchangeable parts.
- a. Participatory management
- b. Human relations
- c. Hersey-Blanchard situational theory
- d. Work design

14. _____ refers to those researchers of organizational development who study the behavior of people in groups, in particular workplace groups. It originated in the 1920s' Hawthorne studies, which examined the effects of social relations, motivation and employee satisfaction on factory productivity. The movement viewed workers in terms of their psychology and fit with companies, rather than as interchangeable parts.
- a. Path-goal theory
- b. Job satisfaction
- c. Job analysis
- d. Human relations movement

15. _____ and Theory Y are theories of human motivation created and developed by Douglas McGregor at the MIT Sloan School of Management in the 1960s that have been used in human resource management, organizational behavior, organizational communication and organizational development. They describe two very different attitudes toward workforce motivation. McGregor felt that companies followed either one or the other approach.

In _____, which many managers practice, management assumes employees are inherently lazy and will avoid work if they can. They inherently dislike work. Because of this, workers need to be closely supervised and comprehensive systems of controls developed.

- a. Job enrichment
- b. Management team
- c. Cash cow
- d. Theory X

16. Theory X and _____ are theories of human motivation created and developed by Douglas McGregor at the MIT Sloan School of Management in the 1960s that have been used in human resource management, organizational behavior, organizational communication and organizational development. They describe two very different attitudes toward workforce motivation. McGregor felt that companies followed either one or the other approach.

In _____, management assumes employees may be ambitious and self-motivated and exercise self-control. It is believed that employees enjoy their mental and physical work duties.

- a. Theory Y
- b. Contingency theory
- c. Design leadership
- d. Business Workflow Analysis

Chapter 2. Management Theory: Essential Background for the Successful Manager

17. Maslow's _____ is a theory in psychology, proposed by Abraham Maslow in his 1943 paper A Theory of Human Motivation, which he subsequently extended to include his observations of humans' innate curiosity.

Maslow's _____ is predetermined in order of importance. It is often depicted as a pyramid consisting of five levels: the lowest level is associated with physiological needs, while the uppermost level is associated with self-actualization needs, particularly those related to identity and purpose. Deficiency needs must be met first. Once these are met, seeking to satisfy growth needs drives personal growth. The higher needs in this hierarchy only come into focus when the lower needs in the pyramid are met.

- a. 1990 Clean Air Act
- b. 28-hour day
- c. 33 Strategies of War
- d. Hierarchy of needs

18. _____ can be regarded as an outcome of mental processes (cognitive process) leading to the selection of a course of action among several alternatives. Every _____ process produces a final choice. The output can be an action or an opinion of choice.
- a. 28-hour day
- b. 33 Strategies of War
- c. 1990 Clean Air Act
- d. Decision making

19. _____, is the discipline of using scientific research-based principles, strategies, and other analytical methods, such as mathematical modeling to improve any organization's ability to enact rational, meaningful business management decisions.
- a. Trustee
- b. Workflow
- c. Management science
- d. Cross ownership

20. _____ in the USA, Canada, South Africa and Australia, and operational research in Europe, is an interdisciplinary branch of applied mathematics and formal science that uses methods such as mathematical modeling, statistics, and algorithms to arrive at optimal or near optimal solutions to complex problems. It is typically concerned with optimizing the maxima (profit, assembly line performance, crop yield, bandwidth, etc) or minima (loss, risk, etc.) of some objective function.
- a. AAAI
- b. A4e
- c. A Stake in the Outcome
- d. Operations research

21. _____ is an inventory strategy that strives to improve the return on investment of a business by reducing in-process inventory and its associated carrying costs. To meet _____ objectives, the process relies on signals between different points in the process. This means the process is often driven by a series of signals, or Kanban , which tell production when to make the next part. Kanban are usually 'tickets' but can be simple visual signals, such as the presence or absence of a part on a shelf. Implemented correctly, _____ can dramatically improve a manufacturing organization's return on investment, quality, and efficiency.
- a. 1990 Clean Air Act
- b. 28-hour day
- c. 33 Strategies of War
- d. Just-in-time

22. _____ is an area of business concerned with the production of goods and services, and involves the responsibility of ensuring that business operations are efficient in terms of using as little resource as needed, and effective in terms of meeting customer requirements. It is concerned with managing the process that converts inputs (in the forms of materials, labour and energy) into outputs (in the form of goods and services.)

Chapter 2. Management Theory: Essential Background for the Successful Manager

Operations traditionally refers to the production of goods and services separately, although the distinction between these two main types of operations is increasingly difficult to make as manufacturers tend to merge product and service offerings.

- a. A Stake in the Outcome
- b. A4e
- c. AAAI
- d. Operations management

23. _____ refers to planned and systematic production processes that provide confidence in a product's suitability for its intended purpose. Refer to the definition by Merriam-Webster for further information . It is a set of activities intended to ensure that products (goods and/or services) satisfy customer requirements in a systematic, reliable fashion.
   - a. 1990 Clean Air Act
   - b. Risk assessment
   - c. 28-hour day
   - d. Quality assurance

24. In engineering and manufacturing, _____ and quality engineering are used in developing systems to ensure products or services are designed and produced to meet or exceed customer requirements. Refer to the definition by Merriam-Webster for further information . These systems are often developed in conjunction with other business and engineering disciplines using a cross-functional approach.
   - a. Statistical process control
   - b. Quality control
   - c. Process capability
   - d. Single Minute Exchange of Die

25. _____ is a business management strategy aimed at embedding awareness of quality in all organizational processes. _____ has been widely used in manufacturing, education, hospitals, call centers, government, and service industries, as well as NASA space and science programs.

As defined by the International Organization for Standardization (ISO):

'_____ is a management approach for an organization, centered on quality, based on the participation of all its members and aiming at long-term success through customer satisfaction, and benefits to all members of the organization and to society.' ISO 8402:1994

One major aim is to reduce variation from every process so that greater consistency of effort is obtained. (Royse, D., Thyer, B., Padgett D., ' Logan T., 2006)

- a. 1990 Clean Air Act
- b. Total quality management
- c. 28-hour day
- d. Quality management

26. _____ can be considered to have three main components: quality control, quality assurance and quality improvement. _____ is focused not only on product quality, but also the means to achieve it. _____ therefore uses quality assurance and control of processes as well as products to achieve more consistent quality.
   - a. 28-hour day
   - b. Total quality management
   - c. 1990 Clean Air Act
   - d. Quality management

27. _____ describes the situation when output from (or information about the result of) an event or phenomenon in the past will influence the same event/phenomenon in the present or future. When an event is part of a chain of cause-and-effect that forms a circuit or loop, then the event is said to 'feed back' into itself.

Chapter 2. Management Theory: Essential Background for the Successful Manager

_____ is also a synonym for:

- _____ signal; the information about the initial event that is the basis for subsequent modification of the event.
- _____ loop; the causal path that leads from the initial generation of the _____ signal to the subsequent modification of the event.

_____ is a mechanism, process or signal that is looped back to control a system within itself. Such a loop is called a _____ loop.

  a. Feedback   b. Positive feedback
  c. Feedback loop   d. 1990 Clean Air Act

28. In management science, operations research and organizational development (OD), human organizations are viewed as systems (conceptual systems) of interacting components such as _____ or system aggregates, which are carriers of numerous complex processes and organizational structures. Organizational development theorist Peter Senge developed the notion of organizations as systems in his book The Fifth Discipline.

Systems thinking is a style of thinking/reasoning and problem solving.

  a. 1990 Clean Air Act   b. Subsystems
  c. Systems thinking   d. 28-hour day

29. Generation Y is a term used to describe the demographic cohort following Generation X. Its members are often referred to as 'Millennials' or 'Echo Boomers') . There are no precise dates for when _____ begins and ends. Most commentators use dates from the early 1980s to early 1990s.
  a. Jagdish Natwarlal Bhagwati   b. David C. Korten
  c. Geoffrey Colvin   d. Gen Y

30. _____, commonly abbreviated to Gen X, is a term used to refer to a generational cohort of children born after the baby boom ended and usually prior to the 1980s

The term _____ has been used in demography, the social sciences, and marketing, though it is most often used in popular culture.

In the U.S. _____ was originally referred to as the 'baby bust' generation because of the drop in the birth rate following the baby boom.

  a. Abraham Harold Maslow   b. Adam Smith
  c. Generation X   d. Affiliation

31. _____ is a term used to describe the demographic cohort following Generation X. Its members are often referred to as 'Millennials' or 'Echo Boomers') . There are no precise dates for when Gen Y begins and ends. Most commentators use dates from the early 1980s to early 1990s.

a. David Wittig
b. Benjamin R. Barber
c. Giovanni Agnelli
d. Generation Y

32. _____ is the process of extracting hidden patterns from data. As more data is gathered, with the amount of data doubling every three years, _____ is becoming an increasingly important tool to transform this data into information. It is commonly used in a wide range of profiling practices, such as marketing, surveillance, fraud detection and scientific discovery.
   a. Decision tree learning
   b. Data mining
   c. 1990 Clean Air Act
   d. 28-hour day

33. _____ is a mathematical science pertaining to the collection, analysis, interpretation or explanation, and presentation of data. It also provides tools for prediction and forecasting based on data. It is applicable to a wide variety of academic disciplines, from the natural and social sciences to the humanities, government and business.
   a. Location parameter
   b. Failure rate
   c. Simple moving average
   d. Statistics

34. _____ is the process of comparing the cost, cycle time, productivity, or quality of a specific process or method to another that is widely considered to be an industry standard or best practice. Essentially, _____ provides a snapshot of the performance of your business and helps you understand where you are in relation to a particular standard. The result is often a business case for making changes in order to make improvements.
   a. Benchmarking
   b. Cost leadership
   c. Competitive heterogeneity
   d. Complementors

35. In probability theory, a probability distribution is called _____ if its cumulative distribution function is _____. This is equivalent to saying that for random variables X with the distribution in question, Pr[X = a] = 0 for all real numbers a, i.e.: the probability that X attains the value a is zero, for any number a. If the distribution of X is _____ then X is called a _____ random variable.
   a. Pay Band
   b. Decision tree pruning
   c. Connectionist expert systems
   d. Continuous

36. _____ is a management process whereby delivery (customer valued) processes are constantly evaluated and improved in the light of their efficiency, effectiveness and flexibility.

Some see it as a meta process for most management systems (Business Process Management, Quality Management, Project Management). Deming saw it as part of the 'system' whereby feedback from the process and customer were evaluated against organisational goals.

   a. Sole proprietorship
   b. Critical Success Factor
   c. Continuous Improvement Process
   d. First-mover advantage

37. _____ is the strategic and coherent approach to the management of an organisation's most valued assets - the people working there who individually and collectively contribute to the achievement of the objectives of the business. The terms '_____' and 'human resources' (HR) have largely replaced the term 'personnel management' as a description of the processes involved in managing people in organizations. In simple sense, _____ means employing people, developing their resources, utilizing, maintaining and compensating their services in tune with the job and organizational requirement.

Chapter 2. Management Theory: Essential Background for the Successful Manager

a. Human resource management
b. Progressive discipline
c. Revolving door syndrome
d. Job knowledge

38. _____ is a method by which the job performance of an employee is evaluated _____ is a part of career development.

_____s are regular reviews of employee performance within organizations

Generally, the aims of a _____ are to:

- Give feedback on performance to employees.
- Identify employee training needs.
- Document criteria used to allocate organizational rewards.
- Form a basis for personnel decisions: salary increases, promotions, disciplinary actions, etc.
- Provide the opportunity for organizational diagnosis and development.
- Facilitate communication between employee and administraton
- Validate selection techniques and human resource policies to meet federal Equal Employment Opportunity requirements.

A common approach to assessing performance is to use a numerical or scalar rating system whereby managers are asked to score an individual against a number of objectives/attributes. In some companies, employees receive assessments from their manager, peers, subordinates and customers while also performing a self assessment.

a. Human resource management
b. Personnel management
c. Progressive discipline
d. Performance appraisal

39. _____ in its literal sense is the process of transformation of local or regional phenomena into global ones. It can be described as a process by which the people of the world are unified into a single society and function together.

This process is a combination of economic, technological, sociocultural and political forces.

a. Histogram
b. Globalization
c. Collaborative Planning, Forecasting and Replenishment
d. Cost Management

40. A _____ is a contemporary apporach to organizational design. It is an organization that is not defined by, or limited to, the horizontal, vertical, or external boundaries imposed by a predefined structure. This term was coined by former GE chairman Jack Welch because he wanted to eliminate vertical and horizontal boundaries within GE and break down external barriers between the company and its customers and suppliers.

a. Chief risk officer
b. Headquarters
c. Business Roundtable
d. Boundaryless organization

41. _____ refers to the stock of skills and knowledge embodied in the ability to perform labor so as to produce economic value. It is the skills and knowledge gained by a worker through education and experience. Many early economic theories refer to it simply as labor, one of three factors of production, and consider it to be a fungible resource -- homogeneous and easily interchangeable.
   a. Market structure
   b. Deflation
   c. Productivity management
   d. Human capital

42. A _____ in today's workforce is an individual that is valued for their ability to interpret information within a specific subject area. They will often advance the overall understanding of that subject through focused analysis, design and/or development. They use research skills to define problems and to identify alternatives.
   a. Career development
   b. Customer satisfaction
   c. Business rule
   d. Knowledge worker

43. _____ is a form of communication that typically attempts to persuade potential customers to purchase or to consume more of a particular brand of product or service. 'While now central to the contemporary global economy and the reproduction of global production networks, it is only quite recently that _____ has been more than a marginal influence on patterns of sales and production. The formation of modern _____ was intimately bound up with the emergence of new forms of monopoly capitalism around the end of the 19th and beginning of the 20th century as one element in corporate strategies to create, organize and where possible control markets, especially for mass produced consumer goods.
   a. Advertising
   b. A Stake in the Outcome
   c. AAAI
   d. A4e

44. _____ is a group creativity technique designed to generate a large number of ideas for the solution of a problem. The method was first popularized in the late 1930s by Alex Faickney Osborn in a book called Applied Imagination. Osborn proposed that groups could double their creative output with _____.
   a. Brainstorming
   b. Affiliation
   c. Abraham Harold Maslow
   d. Adam Smith

45. In economics, a _____ exists when a specific individual or enterprise has sufficient control over a particular product or service to determine significantly the terms on which other individuals shall have access to it. Monopolies are thus characterized by a lack of economic competition for the good or service that they provide and a lack of viable substitute goods. The verb 'monopolize' refers to the process by which a firm gains persistently greater market share than what is expected under perfect competition.
   a. 33 Strategies of War
   b. 28-hour day
   c. Monopoly
   d. 1990 Clean Air Act

Chapter 3. The Manager's Changing Work Environment & Ethical Responsibilities

1. _____ is the strategic and coherent approach to the management of an organisation's most valued assets - the people working there who individually and collectively contribute to the achievement of the objectives of the business. The terms '_____' and 'human resources' (HR) have largely replaced the term 'personnel management' as a description of the processes involved in managing people in organizations. In simple sense, _____ means employing people, developing their resources, utilizing, maintaining and compensating their services in tune with the job and organizational requirement.
 a. Job knowledge   b. Progressive discipline
 c. Revolving door syndrome   d. Human resource management

2. _____ is a management technique pioneered by Michael Phillips in San Francisco in the late '60's and early '70s. The concept's most visible success was by Jack Stack and his team at SRC Holdings and popularized in 1995 by John Case. The technique is to give employees all relevant financial information about the company so they can make better decisions as workers.
 a. AAAI   b. Open-book management
 c. A4e   d. A Stake in the Outcome

3. _____ is a method by which the job performance of an employee is evaluated _____ is a part of career development.

_____s are regular reviews of employee performance within organizations

Generally, the aims of a _____ are to:

- Give feedback on performance to employees.
- Identify employee training needs.
- Document criteria used to allocate organizational rewards.
- Form a basis for personnel decisions: salary increases, promotions, disciplinary actions, etc.
- Provide the opportunity for organizational diagnosis and development.
- Facilitate communication between employee and administraton
- Validate selection techniques and human resource policies to meet federal Equal Employment Opportunity requirements.

A common approach to assessing performance is to use a numerical or scalar rating system whereby managers are asked to score an individual against a number of objectives/attributes. In some companies, employees receive assessments from their manager, peers, subordinates and customers while also performing a self assessment.

 a. Progressive discipline   b. Personnel management
 c. Human resource management   d. Performance appraisal

4. In a human resources context, _____ or labor _____ is the rate at which an employer gains and loses employees. Simple ways to describe it are 'how long employees tend to stay' or 'the rate of traffic through the revolving door.' _____ is measured for individual companies and for their industry as a whole. If an employer is said to have a high _____ relative to its competitors, it means that employees of that company have a shorter average tenure than those of other companies in the same industry.
 a. Career portfolios   b. Ten year occupational employment projection
 c. Continuous   d. Turnover

Chapter 3. The Manager's Changing Work Environment & Ethical Responsibilities

5. A _____ is a type of business entity in which partners (owners) share with each other the profits or losses of the business. _____s are often favored over corporations for taxation purposes, as the _____ structure does not generally incur a tax on profits before it is distributed to the partners (i.e. there is no dividend tax levied.) However, depending on the _____ structure and the jurisdiction in which it operates, owners of a _____ may be exposed to greater personal liability than they would as shareholders of a corporation.
   a. Partnership
   b. Federal Employers Liability Act
   c. Due process
   d. Mediation

6. A _____ also known as a sole trader, or simply proprietorship is a type of business entity which there is only one owner and he has the final word taking all desicions by himself. All debts of the business are debts of the owner and must pay from his personal possessions. This means that the owner has unlimited liabilty.
   a. Foreign ownership
   b. Sole proprietorship
   c. Business rule
   d. Golden hello

7. A mutual shareholder or _____ is an individual or company (including a corporation) that legally owns one or more shares of stock in a joint stock company. A company's shareholders collectively own that company. Thus, the typical goal of such companies is to enhance shareholder value.
   a. Free riding
   b. Shareholder
   c. 1990 Clean Air Act
   d. Stockholder

8. _____ is a legal term that refers to a holder of property on behalf of a beneficiary. A trust can be set up either to benefit particular persons, or for any charitable purposes (but not generally for non-charitable purposes): typical examples are a will trust for the testator's children and family, a pension trust (to confer benefits on employees and their families), and a charitable trust. In all cases, the _____ may be a person or company, whether or not they are a prospective beneficiary.
   a. Commercial management
   b. Trustee
   c. Hierarchical organization
   d. Design management

9. _____ is the state or fact of exclusive rights and control over property, which may be an object, land/real estate or intellectual property. An _____ right is also referred to as title. The concept of _____ has existed for thousands of years and in all cultures.
   a. A Stake in the Outcome
   b. Emanation of the state
   c. A4e
   d. Ownership

10. _____ is subcontracting a process, such as product design or manufacturing, to a third-party company. The decision to outsource is often made in the interest of lowering cost or making better use of time and energy costs, redirecting or conserving energy directed at the competencies of a particular business, or to make more efficient use of land, labor, capital, (information) technology and resources. _____ became part of the business lexicon during the 1980s.
    a. Operant conditioning
    b. Unemployment insurance
    c. Opinion leadership
    d. Outsourcing

11. _____ is a concept related to the relative abilities of parties in a situation to exert influence over each other. If both parties are on an equal footing in a debate, then they will have equal _____, such as in a perfectly competitive market, or between an evenly matched monopoly and monopsony.

There are a number of fields where the concept of _____ has proven crucial to coherent analysis: game theory, labour economics, collective bargaining arrangements, diplomatic negotiations, settlement of litigation, the price of insurance, and any negotiation in general.

a. 1990 Clean Air Act
b. Buy-sell agreement
c. Trade credit
d. Bargaining power

12. _____ is the sum of all experiences a customer has with a supplier of goods or services, over the duration of their relationship with that supplier. It can also be used to mean an individual experience over one transaction; the distinction is usually clear in context.

Analysts and commentators who write about _____ and CRM have increasingly recognized the importance of managing the customer's experience.

a. 28-hour day
b. Customer service
c. 1990 Clean Air Act
d. Customer experience

13. _____ is the provision of service to customers before, during and after a purchase.

According to Turban et al. (2002), '_____ is a series of activities designed to enhance the level of customer satisfaction - that is, the feeling that a product or service has met the customer expectation.'

Its importance varies by product, industry and customer; defective or broken merchandise can be exchanged, often only with a receipt and within a specified time frame.

a. 1990 Clean Air Act
b. 28-hour day
c. Service rate
d. Customer service

14. _____ is one of the four elements of marketing mix. An organization or set of organizations (go-betweens) involved in the process of making a product or service available for use or consumption by a consumer or business user.

The other three parts of the marketing mix are product, pricing, and promotion.

a. Missing completely at random
b. Distribution
c. Job creation programs
d. Matching theory

15. _____ is an integrated communications-based process through which individuals and communities discover that existing and newly-identified needs and wants may be satisfied by the products and services of others.

_____ is defined by the American _____ Association as the activity, set of institutions, and processes for creating, communicating, delivering, and exchanging offerings that have value for customers, clients, partners, and society at large. The term developed from the original meaning which referred literally to going to market, as in shopping, or going to a market to buy or sell goods or services.

Chapter 3. The Manager's Changing Work Environment & Ethical Responsibilities

a. Customer relationship management
b. Market development
c. Disruptive technology
d. Marketing

16. A _____ is a process that can allow an organization to concentrate its limited resources on the greatest opportunities to increase sales and achieve a sustainable competitive advantage. A _____ should be centered around the key concept that customer satisfaction is the main goal.

A _____ is a written plan which combines product development, promotion, distribution, and pricing approach, identifies the firm's marketing goals, and explains how they will be achieved within a stated timeframe.

a. Category management
b. Disruptive technology
c. Marketing strategy
d. Product bundling

17. _____ is an advertisement in which a particular product specifically mentions a competitor by name for the express purpose of showing why the competitor is inferior to the product naming it.

This should not be confused with parody advertisements, where a fictional product is being advertised for the purpose of poking fun at the particular advertisement, nor should it be confused with the use of a coined brand name for the purpose of comparing the product without actually naming an actual competitor. ('Wikipedia tastes better and is less filling than the Encyclopedia Galactica.')

In the 1980s, during what has been referred to as the cola wars, soft-drink manufacturer Pepsi ran a series of advertisements where people, caught on hidden camera, in a blind taste test, chose Pepsi over rival Coca-Cola.

a. 1990 Clean Air Act
b. 33 Strategies of War
c. Comparative advertising
d. 28-hour day

18. A _____ is a working environment with conditions that are considered by many people of industrialized nations to be difficult or dangerous, usually where the workers have few opportunities to address their situation. This can include exposure to harmful materials, hazardous situations, extreme temperatures, or abuse from employers. _____ workers often work long hours for little pay, regardless of any laws mandating overtime pay or a minimum wage.

a. Continuous
b. Complement
c. Rate of return
d. Sweatshop

19. The _____ is an international organization designed by its founders to supervise and liberalize international trade. The organization officially commenced on 1 January 1995, under the Marrakesh Agreement, succeeding the 1947 General Agreement on Tariffs and Trade (GATT.)

The _____ deals with regulation of trade between participating countries; it provides a framework for negotiating and formalising trade agreements, and a dispute resolution process aimed at enforcing participants' adherence to _____ agreements which are signed by representatives of member governments and ratified by their parliaments.

Chapter 3. The Manager's Changing Work Environment & Ethical Responsibilities

a. 1990 Clean Air Act
b. World Trade Organization
c. Network planning and design
d. National Institute for Occupational Safety and Health

20. _____ refers to metrics and measures of output from production processes, per unit of input. Labor _____, for example, is typically measured as a ratio of output per labor-hour, an input. _____ may be conceived of as a metrics of the technical or engineering efficiency of production.
   a. Master production schedule
   b. Remanufacturing
   c. Value engineering
   d. Productivity

21. _____ is one of the managerial functions like planning, organizing, staffing and directing. It is an important function because it helps to check the errors and to take the corrective action so that deviation from standards are minimized and stated goals of the organization are achieved in desired manner. According to modern concepts, _____ is a foreseeing action whereas earlier concept of _____ was used only when errors were detected. _____ in management means setting standards, measuring actual performance and taking corrective action.
   a. Schedule of reinforcement
   b. Decision tree pruning
   c. Turnover
   d. Control

22. _____ is the temporary suspension or permanent termination of employment of an employee or (more commonly) a group of employees for business reasons, such as the decision that certain positions are no longer necessary or a business slow-down or interruption in work. Originally the term '_____' referred exclusively to a temporary interruption in work, as when factory work cyclically falls off. However, in recent times the term can also refer to the permanent elimination of a position.
   a. Retirement
   b. Wrongful dismissal
   c. Termination of employment
   d. Layoff

23. _____ or _____ data refers to selected population characteristics as used in government, marketing or opinion research, or the _____ profiles used in such research. Note the distinction from the term 'demography' Commonly-used _____s include race, age, income, disabilities, mobility (in terms of travel time to work or number of vehicles available), educational attainment, home ownership, employment status, and even location.
   a. Affiliation
   b. Adam Smith
   c. Abraham Harold Maslow
   d. Demographic

24. _____ is an idea in the field of Organizational studies and management which describes the psychology, attitudes, experiences, beliefs and Values (personal and cultural values) of an organization. It has been defined as 'the specific collection of values and norms that are shared by people and groups in an organization and that control the way they interact with each other and with stakeholders outside the organization.'

This definition continues to explain organizational values also known as 'beliefs and ideas about what kinds of goals members of an organization should pursue and ideas about the appropriate kinds or standards of behavior organizational members should use to achieve these goals. From organizational values develop organizational norms, guidelines or expectations that prescribe appropriate kinds of behavior by employees in particular situations and control the behavior of organizational members towards one another.'

_____ is not the same as corporate culture.

Chapter 3. The Manager's Changing Work Environment & Ethical Responsibilities 27

a. Union shop
b. Organizational development
c. Organizational effectiveness
d. Organizational culture

25. In economics, a _____ exists when a specific individual or enterprise has sufficient control over a particular product or service to determine significantly the terms on which other individuals shall have access to it. Monopolies are thus characterized by a lack of economic competition for the good or service that they provide and a lack of viable substitute goods. The verb 'monopolize' refers to the process by which a firm gains persistently greater market share than what is expected under perfect competition.
   a. 28-hour day
   b. 1990 Clean Air Act
   c. 33 Strategies of War
   d. Monopoly

26. The term '_____' refers to the concept of collecting information and attempting to spot a pattern in the information. In some fields of study, the term '_____' has more formally-defined meanings.

In project management _____ is a mathematical technique that uses historical results to predict future outcome.

   a. Least squares
   b. Trend analysis
   c. Stepwise regression
   d. Regression analysis

27. An _____ is a situation that will often involve an apparent conflict between moral imperatives, in which to obey one would result in transgressing another. This is also called an ethical paradox since in moral philosophy, paradox plays a central role in ethics debates. For instance, an ethical admonition to 'love thy neighbour as thy self' is not always just in contrast with, but sometimes in contradiction to an armed neighbour actively trying to kill you: if he or she succeeds, you will not be able to love him or her.
   a. A Stake in the Outcome
   b. A4e
   c. Ethical dilemma
   d. AAAI

28. A _____ is a set of consistent ethic values (more specifically the personal and cultural values) and measures used for the purpose of ethical or ideological integrity. A well defined _____ is a moral code.

Fred Wenst>øp and Arild Myrmel have proposed a structure for corporate _____s that consists of three value categories. These are considered complementary and juxtaposed on the same level if illustrated graphically on for instance an organization's web page. The first value category is Core Values, which prescribe the attitude and character of an organization, and are often found in sections on Code of conduct on its web page. The philosophical antecedents of these values are Virtue ethics, which is often attributed to Aristotle. Protected Values are protected through rules, standards and certifications. They are often concerned with areas such as health, environment and safety. The third category, Created Values, is the values that stakeholders, including the shareholders expect in return for their contributions to the firm. These values are subject to trade-off by decision-makers or bargaining processes. This process is explained further in Stakeholder theory.

   a. 1990 Clean Air Act
   b. Value system
   c. 33 Strategies of War
   d. 28-hour day

29. A _____ or chief executive is one of the highest-ranking corporate officer (executive) or administrator in charge of total management. An individual selected as President and _____ of a corporation, company, organization, or agency, reports to the board of directors. In internal communication and press releases, many companies capitalize the term and those of other high positions, even when they are not proper nouns.
   a. Financial analyst
   b. Purchasing manager
   c. Chief executive officer
   d. Chief brand officer

30. The _____ of a company or public agency is the corporate officer primarily responsible for managing the financial risks of the business or agency. This officer is also responsible for financial planning and record-keeping, as well as financial reporting to higher management. (In recent years, however, the role has expanded to encompass communicating financial performance and forecasts to the analyst community.)
   a. 1990 Clean Air Act
   b. 33 Strategies of War
   c. 28-hour day
   d. Chief financial officer

31. _____ are formal records of the financial activities of a business, person, or other entity. In British English, including United Kingdom company law, _____ are often referred to as accounts, although the term _____ is also used, particularly by accountants.

   _____ provide an overview of a business or person's financial condition in both short and long term.

   a. Financial statements
   b. 1990 Clean Air Act
   c. 28-hour day
   d. 33 Strategies of War

32. In economics and sociology, an _____ is any factor (financial or non-financial) that enables or motivates a particular course of action, or counts as a reason for preferring one choice to the alternatives. It is an expectation that encourages people to behave in a certain way. Since human beings are purposeful creatures, the study of _____ structures is central to the study of all economic activity (both in terms of individual decision-making and in terms of co-operation and competition within a larger institutional structure.)
   a. Incentive
   b. AAAI
   c. A Stake in the Outcome
   d. A4e

33. The _____ of 2002 (Pub.L. 107-204, 116 Stat. 745, enacted July 30, 2002), also known as the Public Company Accounting Reform and Investor Protection Act of 2002 and commonly called Sarbanes-Oxley, Sarbox or SOX, is a United States federal law enacted on July 30, 2002, as a reaction to a number of major corporate and accounting scandals including those affecting Enron, Tyco International, Adelphia, Peregrine Systems and WorldCom.
   a. Letter of credit
   b. Sarbanes-Oxley Act
   c. Sarbanes-Oxley Act of 2002
   d. Fair Labor Standards Act

34. While _____ literally refers to a person responsible for the performance of duties involved in running an organization, the exact meaning of the role is variable, depending on the organization.

While there is no clear line between executive or principal and inferior officers, principal officers are high-level officials in the executive branch of U.S. government such as department heads of independent agencies. In Humphrey's Executor v. United States, 295 U.S. 602 (1935), the Court distinguished between _____s and quasi-legislative or quasi-judicial officers by stating that the former serve at the pleasure of the President and may be removed at his discretion.

Chapter 3. The Manager's Changing Work Environment & Ethical Responsibilities

a. Executive officer
b. Unreported employment
c. Australian Fair Pay and Conditions Standard
d. Easement

35. Engineering _____ is the permissible limit of variation in

   1. a physical dimension,
   2. a measured value or physical property of a material, manufactured object, system, or service,
   3. other measured values (such as temperature, humidity, etc.)
   4. in engineering and safety, a physical distance or space (_____), as in a truck (lorry), train or boat under a bridge as well as a train in a tunnel

Dimensions, properties, or conditions may vary within certain practical limits without significantly affecting functioning of equipment or a process. _____s are specified to allow reasonable leeway for imperfections and inherent variability without compromising performance.

The _____ may be specified as a factor or percentage of the nominal value, a maximum deviation from a nominal value, an explicit range of allowed values, be specified by a note or published standard with this information, or be implied by the numeric accuracy of the nominal value. _____ can be symmetrical, as in 40±0.1, or asymmetrical, such as 40+0.2/−0.1.

a. Root cause analysis
b. Quality assurance
c. Zero defects
d. Tolerance

36. _____ is the act by an employer of terminating employment. Though such a decision can be made by an employer for a variety of reasons, ranging from an economic downturn to performance-related problems on the part of the employee, being fired has a strong stigma in many cultures. To be fired, as opposed to quitting voluntarily (or being laid off), is often perceived as being the employee's fault, and is therefore considered to be disgraceful and a sign of failure.

a. Firing
b. Layoff
c. Severance package
d. Termination of employment

37. _____ is a cross-disciplinary area concerned with protecting the safety, health and welfare of people engaged in work or employment. The goal of all _____ programs is to foster a work free safe environment. As a secondary effect, it may also protect co-workers, family members, employers, customers, suppliers, nearby communities, and other members of the public who are impacted by the workplace environment.

a. AAAI
b. A4e
c. A Stake in the Outcome
d. Occupational Safety and Health

38. The United States _____ is an agency of the United States Department of Labor. It was created by Congress under the Occupational Safety and Health Act, signed by President Richard M. Nixon, on December 29, 1970. Its mission is to prevent work-related injuries, illnesses, and deaths by issuing and enforcing rules (called standards) for workplace safety and health.

a. Occupational Safety and Health Administration
b. Opinion leadership
c. Operant conditioning
d. Unemployment insurance

Chapter 3. The Manager's Changing Work Environment & Ethical Responsibilities

39. _____ and Theory Y are theories of human motivation created and developed by Douglas McGregor at the MIT Sloan School of Management in the 1960s that have been used in human resource management, organizational behavior, organizational communication and organizational development. They describe two very different attitudes toward workforce motivation. McGregor felt that companies followed either one or the other approach.

In _____, which many managers practice, management assumes employees are inherently lazy and will avoid work if they can. They inherently dislike work. Because of this, workers need to be closely supervised and comprehensive systems of controls developed.

- a. Theory X
- b. Job enrichment
- c. Management team
- d. Cash cow

40. Theory X and _____ are theories of human motivation created and developed by Douglas McGregor at the MIT Sloan School of Management in the 1960s that have been used in human resource management, organizational behavior, organizational communication and organizational development. They describe two very different attitudes toward workforce motivation. McGregor felt that companies followed either one or the other approach.

In _____, management assumes employees may be ambitious and self-motivated and exercise self-control. It is believed that employees enjoy their mental and physical work duties.

- a. Theory Y
- b. Design leadership
- c. Business Workflow Analysis
- d. Contingency theory

41. A _____ is a person who alleges misconduct. More complex definitions may be used, but the issue is that the _____ usually faces reprisal. The misconduct may be classified in many ways; for example, a violation of a law, rule, regulation and/or a direct threat to public interest, such as fraud, health/safety violations, and corruption.
- a. 1990 Clean Air Act
- b. Whistleblower
- c. 33 Strategies of War
- d. 28-hour day

42. The 'business case for _____', theorizes that in a global marketplace, a company that employs a diverse workforce (both men and women, people of many generations, people from ethnically and racially diverse backgrounds etc.) is better able to understand the demographics of the marketplace it serves and is thus better equipped to thrive in that marketplace than a company that has a more limited range of employee demographics.

An additional corollary suggests that a company that supports the _____ of its workforce can also improve employee satisfaction, productivity and retention.

- a. Trademark
- b. Diversity
- c. Virtual team
- d. Kanban

43. Organizational culture is not the same as _____. It is wider and deeper concepts, something that an organization 'is' rather than what it 'has' (according to Buchanan and Huczynski.)

_____ is the total sum of the values, customs, traditions and meanings that make a company unique.

Chapter 3. The Manager's Changing Work Environment & Ethical Responsibilities

a. Corporate culture
b. Job analysis
c. Work design
d. Path-goal theory

44. According to the American Marketing Association, _____ is the marketing of products that are presumed to be environmentally safe. Thus _____ incorporates a broad range of activities, including product modification, changes to the production process, packaging changes, as well as modifying advertising. Yet defining _____ is not a simple task where several meanings intersect and contradict each other; an example of this will be the existence of varying social, environmental and retail definitions attached to this term.
a. Value chain
b. SWOT analysis
c. Market share
d. Green marketing

45. The _____ (Situation, Task, Action, Result) format is a job interview technique used by interviewers to gather all the relevant information about a specific capability that the job requires. This interview format is said to have a higher degree of predictability of future on-the-job performance than the traditional interview.

- Situation: The interviewer wants you to present a recent challenge and situation in which you found yourself.
- Task: What did you have to achieve? The interviewer will be looking to see what you were trying to achieve from the situation.
- Action: What did you do? The interviewer will be looking for information on what you did, why you did it and what were the alternatives.
- Results: What was the outcome of your actions? What did you achieve through your actions and did you meet your objectives. What did you learn from this experience and have you used this learning since?

a. Competency-based job descriptions
b. Rasch models
c. Phrase completion
d. Star

46. _____ is a contract between two parties, one being the employer and the other being the employee. An employee may be defined as: 'A person in the service of another under any contract of hire, express or implied, oral or written, where the employer has the power or right to control and direct the employee in the material details of how the work is to be performed.' Black's Law Dictionary page 471 (5th ed. 1979.)
a. Exit interview
b. Employment rate
c. Employment counsellor
d. Employment

47. In economics, the term _____ refers to situations where the advancement of a qualified person within the hierarchy of an organization is stopped at a lower level because of some form of discrimination, most commonly sexism or racism, but since the term was coined, '_____' has also come to describe the limited advancement of the deaf, blind, disabled, aged and sexual minorities.It is an unofficial, invisible barrier that prevents women and minorities from advancing in businesses.

This situation is referred to as a 'ceiling' as there is a limitation blocking upward advancement, and 'glass' (transparent) because the limitation is not immediately apparent and is normally an unwritten and unofficial policy. This invisible barrier continues to exist, even though there are no explicit obstacles keeping minorities from acquiring advanced job positions - there are no advertisements that specifically say 'no minorities hired at this establishment', nor are there any formal orders that say 'minorities are not qualified' - but they do lie beneath the surface.

Chapter 3. The Manager's Changing Work Environment & Ethical Responsibilities

a. 33 Strategies of War
b. Glass ceiling
c. 28-hour day
d. 1990 Clean Air Act

48. _____ is a form of insurance that provides compensation medical care for employees who are injured in the course of employment, in exchange for mandatory relinquishment of the employee's right to sue his or her employer for the tort of negligence. The tradeoff between assured, limited coverage and lack of recourse outside the worker compensation system is known as 'the compensation bargain.' While plans differ between jurisdictions, provision can be made for weekly payments in place of wages, compensation for economic loss (past and future), reimbursement or payment of medical and like expenses (functioning in this case as a form of health insurance), and benefits payable to the dependents of workers killed during employment (functioning in this case as a form of life insurance.) General damages for pain and suffering, and punitive damages for employer negligence, are generally not available in worker compensation plans.

a. Workers Compensation
b. Professional liability insurance
c. 28-hour day
d. 1990 Clean Air Act

49. The _____ of 1990 (ADA) is the short title of United States (Pub.L. 101-336, 104 Stat. 327, enacted July 26, 1990), codified at 42 U.S.C. § 12101 et seq. It was signed into law on July 26, 1990, by President George H. W. Bush, and later amended with changes effective January 1, 2009. The ADA is a wide-ranging civil rights law that prohibits, under certain circumstances, discrimination based on disability. It affords similar protections against discrimination to Americans with disabilities as the Civil Rights Act of 1964,

a. Employment discrimination
b. Australian labour law
c. Equal Pay Act of 1963
d. Americans with Disabilities Act

50. In economics, the term _____ has three different distinct meanings and applications. While it is related to unemployment, a situation in which a person who is searching for work cannot find a job, in the case of _____, a person is working. All three of the definitions of '_____' involve underutilization of labor that critics say is missed by most official (governmental agency) definitions and measurements of unemployment.

a. Encore career
b. Underemployment
c. Employee handbook
d. Occupational Employment Statistics

51. _____ occurs when a person is available to work and seeking work but currently without work. The prevalence of _____ is usually measured using the _____ rate, which is defined as the percentage of those in the labor force who are unemployed. The _____ rate is also used in economic studies and economic indexes such as the United States' Conference Board's Index of Leading Indicators as a measure of the state of the macroeconomics.

a. Unemployment
b. Employment-to-population ratio
c. Unemployment Convention, 1919
d. Outplacement

52. _____ is, in its simplest form, the practice of favoring members of a historically disadvantaged group at the expense of members of a historically advantaged group.

In the United States, the terms '_____' and 'reverse racism' have been used in past discussions of racial quotas or gender quotas for collegiate admission to government-run educational institutions. Such policies were held to be unconstitutional in the United States, while non-quota race preferences are legal.

a. 1990 Clean Air Act
b. Separate but equal
c. Sexism,
d. Reverse discrimination

Chapter 3. The Manager's Changing Work Environment & Ethical Responsibilities

53. In economics, _____ is the desire to own something and the ability to pay for it. The term _____ signifies the ability or the willingness to buy a particular commodity at a given point of time.

   a. 28-hour day
   b. 1990 Clean Air Act
   c. 33 Strategies of War
   d. Demand

54. _____ is training for the purpose of increasing participants' cultural awareness, knowledge, and skills, which is based on the assumption that the training will benefit an organization by protecting against civil rights violations, increasing the inclusion of different identity groups, and promoting better teamwork.

   _____ has been a controversial issue, due to moral considerations as well as questioned efficiency or even counterproductivity.

   According to Michael Bird, many project managers may feel that they are treading new territory as they lead project teams made of individuals from different cultures, heterogeneous mixes, and differing demographics.

   a. Soft skill
   b. Role conflict
   c. Self-disclosure
   d. Diversity Training

55. _____ is a term defined by the Oxford English Dictionary as an individual's 'course or progress through life '. It is usually considered to pertain to remunerative work (and sometimes also formal education.)

   The etymology of the term is somewhat ironic in that it comes from the Latin word carrera, which means race .

   a. Spatial mismatch
   b. Nursing shortage
   c. Career
   d. Career planning

56. _____ is a structured approach to transitioning individuals, teams, and organizations from a current state to a desired future state. The current definition of _____ includes both organizational _____ processes and individual _____ models, which together are used to manage the people side of change.

   A number of models are available for understanding the transitioning of individuals through the phases of _____ and strengthening organizational development initiative in both government and corporate sectors.

   a. 33 Strategies of War
   b. 28-hour day
   c. Change management
   d. 1990 Clean Air Act

Chapter 4. Global Management: Managing across Borders

1. The 'business case for _____', theorizes that in a global marketplace, a company that employs a diverse workforce (both men and women, people of many generations, people from ethnically and racially diverse backgrounds etc.) is better able to understand the demographics of the marketplace it serves and is thus better equipped to thrive in that marketplace than a company that has a more limited range of employee demographics.

An additional corollary suggests that a company that supports the _____ of its workforce can also improve employee satisfaction, productivity and retention.

    a. Kanban   b. Trademark
    c. Virtual team   d. Diversity

2. _____ is an idea in the field of Organizational studies and management which describes the psychology, attitudes, experiences, beliefs and Values (personal and cultural values) of an organization. It has been defined as 'the specific collection of values and norms that are shared by people and groups in an organization and that control the way they interact with each other and with stakeholders outside the organization.'

This definition continues to explain organizational values also known as 'beliefs and ideas about what kinds of goals members of an organization should pursue and ideas about the appropriate kinds or standards of behavior organizational members should use to achieve these goals. From organizational values develop organizational norms, guidelines or expectations that prescribe appropriate kinds of behavior by employees in particular situations and control the behavior of organizational members towards one another.'

_____ is not the same as corporate culture.

    a. Union shop   b. Organizational development
    c. Organizational effectiveness   d. Organizational culture

3. _____ in its literal sense is the process of transformation of local or regional phenomena into global ones. It can be described as a process by which the people of the world are unified into a single society and function together.

This process is a combination of economic, technological, sociocultural and political forces.

    a. Histogram   b. Cost Management
    c. Collaborative Planning, Forecasting and   d. Globalization
       Replenishment

4. _____ is subcontracting a process, such as product design or manufacturing, to a third-party company. The decision to outsource is often made in the interest of lowering cost or making better use of time and energy costs, redirecting or conserving energy directed at the competencies of a particular business, or to make more efficient use of land, labor, capital, (information) technology and resources. _____ became part of the business lexicon during the 1980s.

    a. Opinion leadership   b. Unemployment insurance
    c. Outsourcing   d. Operant conditioning

5. The term '_____' refers to the concept of collecting information and attempting to spot a pattern in the information. In some fields of study, the term '_____' has more formally-defined meanings.

Chapter 4. Global Management: Managing across Borders

In project management _____ is a mathematical technique that uses historical results to predict future outcome.

a. Stepwise regression
c. Least squares
b. Trend analysis
d. Regression analysis

6. _____ is the removal or simplification of government rules and regulations that constrain the operation of market forces. _____ does not mean elimination of laws against fraud, but eliminating or reducing government control of how business is done, thereby moving toward a more free market.

The stated rationale for '_____' is often that fewer and simpler regulations will lead to a raised level of competitiveness, therefore higher productivity, more efficiency and lower prices overall.

a. Natural rate of unemployment
c. Value added
b. Rehn-Meidner Model
d. Deregulation

7. _____, commonly known as e-commerce, consists of the buying and selling of products or services over electronic systems such as the Internet and other computer networks. The amount of trade conducted electronically has grown extraordinarily with widespread Internet usage. The use of commerce is conducted in this way, spurring and drawing on innovations in electronic funds transfer, supply chain management, Internet marketing, online transaction processing, electronic data interchange (EDI), inventory management systems, and automated data collection systems.

a. Electronic Commerce
c. Online shopping
b. A4e
d. A Stake in the Outcome

8. _____ is the branch of economics that studies the dynamics of exchange rates, foreign investment, and how these affect international trade. It also studies international projects, international investments and capital flows, and trade deficits. It includes the study of futures, options and currency swaps.

a. A Stake in the Outcome
c. AAAI
b. International finance
d. A4e

9. In economics and sociology, an _____ is any factor (financial or non-financial) that enables or motivates a particular course of action, or counts as a reason for preferring one choice to the alternatives. It is an expectation that encourages people to behave in a certain way. Since human beings are purposeful creatures, the study of _____ structures is central to the study of all economic activity (both in terms of individual decision-making and in terms of co-operation and competition within a larger institutional structure.)

a. A Stake in the Outcome
c. AAAI
b. A4e
d. Incentive

10. The phrase _____ refers to the aspect of corporate strategy, corporate finance and management dealing with the buying, selling and combining of different companies that can aid, finance, or help a growing company in a given industry grow rapidly without having to create another business entity.

An acquisition, also known as a takeover or a buyout, is the buying of one company (the 'target') by another. An acquisition may be friendly or hostile.

a. 28-hour day
b. 1990 Clean Air Act
c. 33 Strategies of War
d. Mergers and acquisitions

11. _____ is an advertisement in which a particular product specifically mentions a competitor by name for the express purpose of showing why the competitor is inferior to the product naming it.

This should not be confused with parody advertisements, where a fictional product is being advertised for the purpose of poking fun at the particular advertisement, nor should it be confused with the use of a coined brand name for the purpose of comparing the product without actually naming an actual competitor. ('Wikipedia tastes better and is less filling than the Encyclopedia Galactica.')

In the 1980s, during what has been referred to as the cola wars, soft-drink manufacturer Pepsi ran a series of advertisements where people, caught on hidden camera, in a blind taste test, chose Pepsi over rival Coca-Cola.

a. 1990 Clean Air Act
b. Comparative advertising
c. 28-hour day
d. 33 Strategies of War

12. The phrase mergers and _____s refers to the aspect of corporate strategy, corporate finance and management dealing with the buying, selling and combining of different companies that can aid, finance, or help a growing company in a given industry grow rapidly without having to create another business entity.

An _____, also known as a takeover or a buyout, is the buying of one company (the 'target') by another. An _____ may be friendly or hostile.

a. A Stake in the Outcome
b. A4e
c. AAAI
d. Acquisition

13. A _____ is a process in which a potential employee is evaluated by an employer for prospective employment in their company, organization and was established in the late 16th century.

A _____ typically precedes the hiring decision, and is used to evaluate the candidate. The interview is usually preceded by the evaluation of submitted résumés from interested candidates, then selecting a small number of candidates for interviews.

a. Payrolling
b. Supported employment
c. Split shift
d. Job interview

14. _____ is the strategic and coherent approach to the management of an organisation's most valued assets - the people working there who individually and collectively contribute to the achievement of the objectives of the business. The terms '_____' and 'human resources' (HR) have largely replaced the term 'personnel management' as a description of the processes involved in managing people in organizations. In simple sense, _____ means employing people, developing their resources, utilizing, maintaining and compensating their services in tune with the job and organizational requirement.

a. Human resource management
b. Revolving door syndrome
c. Job knowledge
d. Progressive discipline

15. _____ is a term defined by the Oxford English Dictionary as an individual's 'course or progress through life '. It is usually considered to pertain to remunerative work (and sometimes also formal education.)

The etymology of the term is somewhat ironic in that it comes from the Latin word carrera, which means race .

a. Spatial mismatch
b. Career planning
c. Nursing shortage
d. Career

16. _____ is a contract between two parties, one being the employer and the other being the employee. An employee may be defined as: 'A person in the service of another under any contract of hire, express or implied, oral or written, where the employer has the power or right to control and direct the employee in the material details of how the work is to be performed.' Black's Law Dictionary page 471 (5th ed. 1979.)

a. Employment counsellor
b. Exit interview
c. Employment
d. Employment rate

17. A _____ is a type of business entity in which partners (owners) share with each other the profits or losses of the business. _____s are often favored over corporations for taxation purposes, as the _____ structure does not generally incur a tax on profits before it is distributed to the partners (i.e. there is no dividend tax levied.) However, depending on the _____ structure and the jurisdiction in which it operates, owners of a _____ may be exposed to greater personal liability than they would as shareholders of a corporation.

a. Due process
b. Federal Employers Liability Act
c. Mediation
d. Partnership

18. _____ is an organization's process of defining its strategy and making decisions on allocating its resources to pursue this strategy, including its capital and people. Various business analysis techniques can be used in _____, including SWOT analysis (Strengths, Weaknesses, Opportunities, and Threats) and PEST analysis (Political, Economic, Social, and Technological analysis) or STEER analysis involving Socio-cultural, Technological, Economic, Ecological, and Regulatory factors and EPISTEL (Environment, Political, Informatic, Social, Technological, Economic and Legal)

_____ is the formal consideration of an organization's future course. All _____ deals with at least one of three key questions:

1. 'What do we do?'
2. 'For whom do we do it?'
3. 'How do we excel?'

In business _____, the third question is better phrased 'How can we beat or avoid competition?'. (Bradford and Duncan, page 1.)

a. 1990 Clean Air Act
b. Strategic planning
c. 28-hour day
d. 33 Strategies of War

Chapter 4. Global Management: Managing across Borders

19. In economics, a _____ exists when a specific individual or enterprise has sufficient control over a particular product or service to determine significantly the terms on which other individuals shall have access to it. Monopolies are thus characterized by a lack of economic competition for the good or service that they provide and a lack of viable substitute goods. The verb 'monopolize' refers to the process by which a firm gains persistently greater market share than what is expected under perfect competition.
   - a. 33 Strategies of War
   - b. 28-hour day
   - c. Monopoly
   - d. 1990 Clean Air Act

20. _____ describes the relocation by a company of a business process from one country to another -- typically an operational process, such as manufacturing such as accounting. Even state governments employ _____.

The term is in use in several distinct but closely related ways.
   - a. A Stake in the Outcome
   - b. AAAI
   - c. Offshoring
   - d. A4e

21. _____ Management is the succession of strategies used by management as a product goes through its _____. The conditions in which a product is sold changes over time and must be managed as it moves through its succession of stages.

The _____ goes through many phases, involves many professional disciplines, and requires many skills, tools and processes.
   - a. Strategic Alliance
   - b. Golden handshake
   - c. Job hunting
   - d. Product life cycle

22. _____ is a concept related to the relative abilities of parties in a situation to exert influence over each other. If both parties are on an equal footing in a debate, then they will have equal _____, such as in a perfectly competitive market, or between an evenly matched monopoly and monopsony.

There are a number of fields where the concept of _____ has proven crucial to coherent analysis: game theory, labour economics, collective bargaining arrangements, diplomatic negotiations, settlement of litigation, the price of insurance, and any negotiation in general.
   - a. Trade credit
   - b. 1990 Clean Air Act
   - c. Buy-sell agreement
   - d. Bargaining power

23. A _____ or maquila is a factory that imports materials and equipment on a duty-free and tariff-free basis for assembly or manufacturing and then re-exports the assembled product, usually back to the originating country. A maquila is also referred to as a 'twin plant', or 'in-bond' industry. Nearly half a million Mexicans are employed in _____s.
   - a. 1990 Clean Air Act
   - b. 33 Strategies of War
   - c. 28-hour day
   - d. Maquiladora

24. _____ is a structured approach to transitioning individuals, teams, and organizations from a current state to a desired future state. The current definition of _____ includes both organizational _____ processes and individual _____ models, which together are used to manage the people side of change.

A number of models are available for understanding the transitioning of individuals through the phases of _____ and strengthening organizational development initiative in both government and corporate sectors.

   a. Change management
   b. 33 Strategies of War
   c. 1990 Clean Air Act
   d. 28-hour day

25. In economics, business, retail, and accounting, a _____ is the value of money that has been used up to produce something, and hence is not available for use anymore. In economics, a _____ is an alternative that is given up as a result of a decision. In business, the _____ may be one of acquisition, in which case the amount of money expended to acquire it is counted as _____.

   a. Cost overrun
   b. Cost allocation
   c. Fixed costs
   d. Cost

26. The _____ is a form of reactivity whereby subjects improve an aspect of their behavior being experimentally measured simply in response to the fact that they are being studied, not in response to any particular experimental manipulation.

The term was coined in 1955 by Henry A. Landsberger when analyzing older experiments from 1924-1932 at the Hawthorne Works (outside Chicago.) Hawthorne Works had commissioned a study to see if its workers would become more productive in higher or lower levels of light.

   a. 33 Strategies of War
   b. 1990 Clean Air Act
   c. 28-hour day
   d. Hawthorne effect

27. _____ is exchange of capital, goods, and services across international borders or territories. In most countries, it represents a significant share of gross domestic product (GDP.) While _____ has been present throughout much of history , its economic, social, and political importance has been on the rise in recent centuries.

   a. A4e
   b. A Stake in the Outcome
   c. International trade
   d. AAAI

28. _____ is one of the managerial functions like planning, organizing, staffing and directing. It is an important function because it helps to check the errors and to take the corrective action so that deviation from standards are minimized and stated goals of the organization are achieved in desired manner. According to modern concepts, _____ is a foreseeing action whereas earlier concept of _____ was used only when errors were detected. _____ in management means setting standards, measuring actual performance and taking corrective action.

   a. Decision tree pruning
   b. Schedule of reinforcement
   c. Control
   d. Turnover

29. _____ refers to a person's capability of gaining initial employment, maintaining employment, and obtaining new employment if required (Hillage and Pollard, 1998.) In simple terms, _____ is about being capable of getting and keeping fulfilling work. More comprehensively, _____ is the capability to move self-sufficiently within the labour market to realise potential through sustainable employment.

   a. Employability
   b. Encore career
   c. Occupational Employment Statistics
   d. Exit interview

Chapter 4. Global Management: Managing across Borders

30. _____ is the probability that an individual will keep his or her job; a job with a high level of _____ is such that a person with the job would have a small chance of becoming unemployed.

_____ is dependent on economy, prevailing business conditions, and the individual's personal skills. It has been found that people have more _____ in times of economic expansion and less in times of a recession.

   a. Hygiene factors
   c. Just cause
   b. Multiple careers
   d. Job security

31. _____ is a sub-topic of machine learning. It is 'the act of taking in raw data and taking an action based on the category of the data'. Most research in _____ is about methods for supervised learning and unsupervised learning.
   a. 1990 Clean Air Act
   c. 33 Strategies of War
   b. 28-hour day
   d. Pattern recognition

32. _____ refers to the methods of practicing and using another person's business philosophy. The franchisor grants the independent operator the right to distribute its products, techniques, and trademarks for a percentage of gross monthly sales and a royalty fee. Various tangibles and intangibles such as national or international advertising, training, and other support services are commonly made available by the franchisor.
   a. Franchising
   c. 28-hour day
   b. ServiceMaster
   d. 1990 Clean Air Act

33. A _____ is an entity formed between two or more parties to undertake economic activity together. The parties agree to create a new entity by both contributing equity, and they then share in the revenues, expenses, and control of the enterprise. The venture can be for one specific project only, or a continuing business relationship such as the Fuji Xerox _____.
   a. Meritor Savings Bank v. Vinson
   c. Patent
   b. Civil Rights Act of 1991
   d. Joint venture

34. An _____ is a person who has possession of an enterprise and assumes significant accountability for the inherent risks and the outcome. It is an ambitious leader who combines land, labor, and capital to create and market new goods or services. The term is a loanword from French and was first defined by the Irish economist Richard Cantillon.
   a. Entrepreneur
   c. A Stake in the Outcome
   b. AAAI
   d. A4e

35. _____ is a type of trade policy that allows traders to act and transact without interference from government. Thus, the policy permits trading partners mutual gains from trade, with goods and services produced according to the theory of comparative advantage.

Under a _____ policy, prices are a reflection of true supply and demand, and are the sole determinant of resource allocation.

   a. 1990 Clean Air Act
   c. 33 Strategies of War
   b. 28-hour day
   d. Free trade

36. A _____ is a general term that describes any government policy or regulation that restricts international trade. The barriers can take many forms, including the following terms that include many restrictions in international trade within multiple countries that import and export any items of trade.

- Import duty
- Import licenses
- Export licenses
- Import quotas
- Tariffs
- Subsidies
- Non-tariff barriers to trade
- Voluntary Export Restraints
- Local Content Requirements
- Embargo

Most _____s work on the same principle: the imposition of some sort of cost on trade that raises the price of the traded products. If two or more nations repeatedly use _____s against each other, then a trade war results.

a. Trade creation
c. Customs brokerage
b. Most favoured nation
d. Trade barrier

37. The _____ was the outcome of the failure of negotiating governments to create the International Trade Organization (ITO.) GATT was formed in 1947 and lasted until 1994, when it was replaced by the World Trade Organization. The Bretton Woods Conference had introduced the idea for an organization to regulate trade as part of a larger plan for economic recovery after World War II.

a. Multilateral treaty
c. General Agreement on Tariffs and Trade
b. 28-hour day
d. 1990 Clean Air Act

38. The _____ is an international organization designed by its founders to supervise and liberalize international trade. The organization officially commenced on 1 January 1995, under the Marrakesh Agreement, succeeding the 1947 General Agreement on Tariffs and Trade (GATT.)

The _____ deals with regulation of trade between participating countries; it provides a framework for negotiating and formalising trade agreements, and a dispute resolution process aimed at enforcing participants' adherence to _____ agreements which are signed by representatives of member governments and ratified by their parliaments.

a. Network planning and design
c. National Institute for Occupational Safety and Health
b. 1990 Clean Air Act
d. World Trade Organization

39. _____ is a designated group of countries that have agreed to eliminate tariffs, quotas and preferences on most (if not all) goods and services traded between them. It can be considered the second stage of economic integration. Countries choose this kind of economic integration form if their economical structures are complementary.

a. 1990 Clean Air Act
b. Free trade area
c. 33 Strategies of War
d. 28-hour day

40. The _____ is a trilateral trade bloc in North America created by the governments of the United States, Canada, and Mexico. The agreement creating the trade bloc came into force on January 1, 1994. It superseded the Canada-United States Free Trade Agreement between the U.S. and Canada.
a. North American Free Trade Agreement
b. Career portfolios
c. Trade union
d. Business war game

41. _____ is a term used to describe any moral, political that stresses human interdependence and the importance of a collective, rather than the importance of separate individuals. Collectivists focus on community and society, and seek to give priority to group goals over individual goals. The philosophical underpinnings of _____ are for some related to holism or organicism - the view that the whole is greater than the sum of its parts/pieces.
a. Collaborative methods
b. 1990 Clean Air Act
c. 28-hour day
d. Collectivism

42. _____ of the learning curve effect and the closely related experience curve effect express the relationship between equations for experience and efficiency or between efficiency gains and investment in the effort. The experience of 'learning curves' was first observed by the 19th Century German psychologist Hermann Ebbinghaus according to the difficulty of memorizing varying numbers of verbal stimuli, and subsequent learning about the complex processes of learning are discussed in the

The rule used for representing the learning curve effect states that the more times a task has been performed, the less time will be required on each subsequent iteration.

a. Models
b. Distribution
c. Point biserial correlation coefficient
d. Spatial Decision Support Systems

43. _____ is a trait taught by many personal development experts and psychotherapists and the subject of many popular self-help books. It is linked to self-esteem and considered an important communication skill.

As a communication style and strategy, _____ is distinguished from aggression and passivity.

a. Assertiveness
b. Intrinsic motivation
c. A Stake in the Outcome
d. A4e

Chapter 4. Global Management: Managing across Borders

44. _____ refers to the movement of cash into or out of a business or financial product. It is usually measured during a specified, finite period of time. Measurement of _____ can be used

- to determine a project's rate of return or value. The time of _____s into and out of projects are used as inputs in financial models such as internal rate of return, and net present value.
- to determine problems with a business's liquidity. Being profitable does not necessarily mean being liquid. A company can fail because of a shortage of cash, even while profitable.
- as an alternate measure of a business's profits when it is believed that accrual accounting concepts do not represent economic realities. For example, a company may be notionally profitable but generating little operational cash (as may be the case for a company that barters its products rather than selling for cash.) In such a case, the company may be deriving additional operating cash by issuing shares evaluating default risk, re-investment requirements, etc.

_____ is a generic term used differently depending on the context. It may be defined by users for their own purposes.

a. Sweat equity
b. Gross profit
c. Gross profit margin
d. Cash flow

45. _____ has been described as the 'process of social influence in which one person can enlist the aid and support of others in the accomplishment of a common task' . A definition more inclusive of followers comes from Alan Keith of Genentech who said '_____ is ultimately about creating a way for people to contribute to making something extraordinary happen.'

_____ is one of the most salient aspects of the organizational context. However, defining _____ has been challenging.

a. Situational leadership
b. 1990 Clean Air Act
c. 28-hour day
d. Leadership

46. _____ is the region surrounding each person, or that area which a person considers their domain or territory. Often if entered by another being without this being desired, it makes them feel uncomfortable. The amount of space a being (person, plant, animal) needs falls into two categories, immediate individual physical space (determined by imagined boundaries), and the space an individual considers theirs to live in (often called habitat.)

a. Personal space
b. Persuasion
c. Machiavellianism
d. Self-enhancement

47. An _____ is a person temporarily or permanently residing in a country and culture other than that of the person's upbringing or legal residence. The word comes from the Latin ex and patria (country, fatherland.)

The term is sometimes used in the context of Westerners living in non-Western countries, although it is also used to describe Westerners living in other Western countries, such as Americans living in the United Kingdom, or Britons living in Spain.

a. A Stake in the Outcome
b. A4e
c. Expatriate
d. AAAI

48. In a human resources context, _____ or labor _____ is the rate at which an employer gains and loses employees. Simple ways to describe it are 'how long employees tend to stay' or 'the rate of traffic through the revolving door.' _____ is measured for individual companies and for their industry as a whole. If an employer is said to have a high _____ relative to its competitors, it means that employees of that company have a shorter average tenure than those of other companies in the same industry.
   a. Career portfolios
   b. Continuous
   c. Ten year occupational employment projection
   d. Turnover

Chapter 5. Planning: The Foundation of Successful Management

1. _____ is a term defined by the Oxford English Dictionary as an individual's 'course or progress through life '. It is usually considered to pertain to remunerative work (and sometimes also formal education.)

The etymology of the term is somewhat ironic in that it comes from the Latin word carrera, which means race .

   a. Career planning
   b. Career
   c. Spatial mismatch
   d. Nursing shortage

2. _____ is the strategic and coherent approach to the management of an organisation's most valued assets - the people working there who individually and collectively contribute to the achievement of the objectives of the business. The terms '_____' and 'human resources' (HR) have largely replaced the term 'personnel management' as a description of the processes involved in managing people in organizations. In simple sense, _____ means employing people, developing their resources, utilizing, maintaining and compensating their services in tune with the job and organizational requirement.

   a. Human resource management
   b. Revolving door syndrome
   c. Job knowledge
   d. Progressive discipline

3. _____ is an organization's process of defining its strategy and making decisions on allocating its resources to pursue this strategy, including its capital and people. Various business analysis techniques can be used in _____, including SWOT analysis (Strengths, Weaknesses, Opportunities, and Threats) and PEST analysis (Political, Economic, Social, and Technological analysis) or STEER analysis involving Socio-cultural, Technological, Economic, Ecological, and Regulatory factors and EPISTEL (Environment, Political, Informatic, Social, Technological, Economic and Legal)

_____ is the formal consideration of an organization's future course. All _____ deals with at least one of three key questions:

   1. 'What do we do?'
   2. 'For whom do we do it?'
   3. 'How do we excel?'

In business _____, the third question is better phrased 'How can we beat or avoid competition?'. (Bradford and Duncan, page 1.)

   a. 33 Strategies of War
   b. Strategic planning
   c. 1990 Clean Air Act
   d. 28-hour day

4. _____ is a subset of career management. _____ applies the concepts of Strategic planning and Marketing to taking charge of one's professional future.
   a. Career Planning
   b. TDY
   c. Forced retention
   d. Military recruitment

5. _____ is one of the managerial functions like planning, organizing, staffing and directing. It is an important function because it helps to check the errors and to take the corrective action so that deviation from standards are minimized and stated goals of the organization are achieved in desired manner. According to modern concepts, _____ is a foreseeing action whereas earlier concept of _____ was used only when errors were detected. _____ in management means setting standards, measuring actual performance and taking corrective action.

a. Turnover
b. Decision tree pruning
c. Schedule of reinforcement
d. Control

6. _____ Management is the succession of strategies used by management as a product goes through its _____. The conditions in which a product is sold changes over time and must be managed as it moves through its succession of stages.

The _____ goes through many phases, involves many professional disciplines, and requires many skills, tools and processes.

a. Strategic Alliance
b. Job hunting
c. Golden handshake
d. Product life cycle

7. A _____ is a brief written statement of the purpose of a company or organization. Ideally, a _____ guides the actions of the organization, spells out its overall goal, provides a sense of direction, and guides decision making for all levels of management.

_____s often contain the following:

- Purpose and aim of the organization
- The organization's primary stakeholders: clients, stockholders, etc.
- Responsibilities of the organization toward these stakeholders
- Products and services offered

In developing a _____:

- Encourage as much input as feasible from employees, volunteers, and other stakeholders
- Publicize it broadly

The _____ can be used to resolve differences between business stakeholders. Stakeholders include: employees including managers and executives, stockholders, board of directors, customers, suppliers, distributors, creditors, governments (local, state, federal, etc.), unions, competitors, NGO's, and the general public.

a. Mission statement
b. 28-hour day
c. 1990 Clean Air Act
d. 33 Strategies of War

8. An _____ is a subset of strategic work plan. It describes short-term ways of achieving milestones and explains how, or what portion of, a strategic plan will be put into operation during a given operational period, in the case of commercial application, a fiscal year or another given budgetary term. An operational plan is the basis for, and justification of an annual operating budget request.

a. A4e
b. A Stake in the Outcome
c. AAAI
d. Operational planning

Chapter 5. Planning: The Foundation of Successful Management

9. In economics and sociology, an _____ is any factor (financial or non-financial) that enables or motivates a particular course of action, or counts as a reason for preferring one choice to the alternatives. It is an expectation that encourages people to behave in a certain way. Since human beings are purposeful creatures, the study of _____ structures is central to the study of all economic activity (both in terms of individual decision-making and in terms of co-operation and competition within a larger institutional structure.)

   a. AAAI
   b. Incentive
   c. A Stake in the Outcome
   d. A4e

10. A _____ is a process in which a potential employee is evaluated by an employer for prospective employment in their company, organization and was established in the late 16th century.

A _____ typically precedes the hiring decision, and is used to evaluate the candidate. The interview is usually preceded by the evaluation of submitted résumés from interested candidates, then selecting a small number of candidates for interviews.

   a. Supported employment
   b. Split shift
   c. Payrolling
   d. Job interview

11. _____ in its literal sense is the process of transformation of local or regional phenomena into global ones. It can be described as a process by which the people of the world are unified into a single society and function together.

This process is a combination of economic, technological, sociocultural and political forces.

   a. Histogram
   b. Collaborative Planning, Forecasting and Replenishment
   c. Cost Management
   d. Globalization

12. _____ is a structured approach to transitioning individuals, teams, and organizations from a current state to a desired future state. The current definition of _____ includes both organizational _____ processes and individual _____ models, which together are used to manage the people side of change.

A number of models are available for understanding the transitioning of individuals through the phases of _____ and strengthening organizational development initiative in both government and corporate sectors.

   a. 28-hour day
   b. 33 Strategies of War
   c. 1990 Clean Air Act
   d. Change management

13. _____ involves establishing specific, measurable and time-targeted objectives. Work on the theory of goal-setting suggests that it's an effective tool for making progress by ensuring that participants in a group with a common goal are clearly aware of what is expected from them if an objective is to be achieved. On a personal level, setting goals is a process that allows people to specify then work towards their own objectives - most commonly with financial or career-based goals.

   a. Catfish effect
   b. Digital strategy
   c. Resource-based view
   d. Goal setting

14. _____ refers to the movement of cash into or out of a business or financial product. It is usually measured during a specified, finite period of time. Measurement of _____ can be used

- to determine a project's rate of return or value. The time of _____s into and out of projects are used as inputs in financial models such as internal rate of return, and net present value.
- to determine problems with a business's liquidity. Being profitable does not necessarily mean being liquid. A company can fail because of a shortage of cash, even while profitable.
- as an alternate measure of a business's profits when it is believed that accrual accounting concepts do not represent economic realities. For example, a company may be notionally profitable but generating little operational cash (as may be the case for a company that barters its products rather than selling for cash.) In such a case, the company may be deriving additional operating cash by issuing shares evaluating default risk, re-investment requirements, etc.

_____ is a generic term used differently depending on the context. It may be defined by users for their own purposes.

a. Gross profit margin
b. Gross profit
c. Sweat equity
d. Cash flow

15. A _____ is a set of instructions having the force of a directive, covering those features of operations that lend themselves to a definite or standardized procedure without loss of effectiveness. Standard Operating Policies and Procedures can be effective catalysts to drive performance improvement and improving organizational results.

a. 1990 Clean Air Act
b. Standard operating procedure
c. Longitudinal study
d. Risk-benefit analysis

16. _____ is a process of agreeing upon objectives within an organization so that management and employees agree to the objectives and understand what they are in the organization.

The term '_____' was first popularized by Peter Drucker in his 1954 book 'The Practice of Management'.

The essence of _____ is participative goal setting, choosing course of actions and decision making.

a. Job enrichment
b. Clean sheet review
c. Business economics
d. Management by objectives

17. _____ is a method by which the job performance of an employee is evaluated _____ is a part of career development.

_____s are regular reviews of employee performance within organizations

Chapter 5. Planning: The Foundation of Successful Management 49

Generally, the aims of a _____ are to:

- Give feedback on performance to employees.
- Identify employee training needs.
- Document criteria used to allocate organizational rewards.
- Form a basis for personnel decisions: salary increases, promotions, disciplinary actions, etc.
- Provide the opportunity for organizational diagnosis and development.
- Facilitate communication between employee and administraton
- Validate selection techniques and human resource policies to meet federal Equal Employment Opportunity requirements.

A common approach to assessing performance is to use a numerical or scalar rating system whereby managers are asked to score an individual against a number of objectives/attributes. In some companies, employees receive assessments from their manager, peers, subordinates and customers while also performing a self assessment.

a. Performance appraisal
c. Human resource management
b. Personnel management
d. Progressive discipline

18. _____ describes the situation when output from (or information about the result of) an event or phenomenon in the past will influence the same event/phenomenon in the present or future. When an event is part of a chain of cause-and-effect that forms a circuit or loop, then the event is said to 'feed back' into itself.

_____ is also a synonym for:

- _____ signal; the information about the initial event that is the basis for subsequent modification of the event.
- _____ loop; the causal path that leads from the initial generation of the _____ signal to the subsequent modification of the event.

_____ is a mechanism, process or signal that is looped back to control a system within itself. Such a loop is called a _____ loop.

a. Positive feedback
c. Feedback
b. 1990 Clean Air Act
d. Feedback loop

19. _____ is subcontracting a process, such as product design or manufacturing, to a third-party company. The decision to outsource is often made in the interest of lowering cost or making better use of time and energy costs, redirecting or conserving energy directed at the competencies of a particular business, or to make more efficient use of land, labor, capital, (information) technology and resources. _____ became part of the business lexicon during the 1980s.

a. Outsourcing
c. Unemployment insurance
b. Operant conditioning
d. Opinion leadership

20. _____ is a concept related to the relative abilities of parties in a situation to exert influence over each other. If both parties are on an equal footing in a debate, then they will have equal _____, such as in a perfectly competitive market, or between an evenly matched monopoly and monopsony.

There are a number of fields where the concept of _____ has proven crucial to coherent analysis: game theory, labour economics, collective bargaining arrangements, diplomatic negotiations, settlement of litigation, the price of insurance, and any negotiation in general.

    a. Buy-sell agreement
    c. 1990 Clean Air Act
    b. Trade credit
    d. Bargaining power

21. A _____ is a change implemented to address a weakness identified in a management system. Normally _____s are implemented in response to a customer complaint, abnormal levels of internal nonconformity, nonconformities identified during an internal audit or adverse or unstable trends in product and process monitoring such as would be identified by SPC.

The process of determining a _____ requires identification of actions that can be taken to prevent or mitigate the weakness.

    a. Zero defects
    c. 1990 Clean Air Act
    b. 28-hour day
    d. Corrective action

22. _____ is an integrated communications-based process through which individuals and communities discover that existing and newly-identified needs and wants may be satisfied by the products and services of others.

_____ is defined by the American _____ Association as the activity, set of institutions, and processes for creating, communicating, delivering, and exchanging offerings that have value for customers, clients, partners, and society at large. The term developed from the original meaning which referred literally to going to market, as in shopping, or going to a market to buy or sell goods or services.

    a. Disruptive technology
    c. Customer relationship management
    b. Market development
    d. Marketing

23. A _____ is a process that can allow an organization to concentrate its limited resources on the greatest opportunities to increase sales and achieve a sustainable competitive advantage. A _____ should be centered around the key concept that customer satisfaction is the main goal.

A _____ is a written plan which combines product development, promotion, distribution, and pricing approach, identifies the firm's marketing goals, and explains how they will be achieved within a stated timeframe.

    a. Product bundling
    c. Disruptive technology
    b. Category management
    d. Marketing strategy

24. _____ is the discipline of planning, organizing and managing resources to bring about the successful completion of specific project goals and objectives. It is often closely related to and sometimes conflated with Program management.

Chapter 5. Planning: The Foundation of Successful Management

A project is a finite endeavor--having specific start and completion dates--undertaken to meet particular goals and objectives, usually to bring about beneficial change or added value.

a. Project engineer
b. Work package
c. Precedence diagram
d. Project management

25. _____ is an idea in the field of Organizational studies and management which describes the psychology, attitudes, experiences, beliefs and Values (personal and cultural values) of an organization. It has been defined as 'the specific collection of values and norms that are shared by people and groups in an organization and that control the way they interact with each other and with stakeholders outside the organization.'

This definition continues to explain organizational values also known as 'beliefs and ideas about what kinds of goals members of an organization should pursue and ideas about the appropriate kinds or standards of behavior organizational members should use to achieve these goals. From organizational values develop organizational norms, guidelines or expectations that prescribe appropriate kinds of behavior by employees in particular situations and control the behavior of organizational members towards one another.'

_____ is not the same as corporate culture.

a. Organizational development
b. Organizational effectiveness
c. Organizational culture
d. Union shop

26. In finance, an _____ is a contract between a buyer and a seller that gives the buyer the right--but not the obligation--to buy or to sell a particular asset (the underlying asset) at a later day at an agreed price. In return for granting the _____, the seller collects a payment (the premium) from the buyer. A call _____ gives the buyer the right to buy the underlying asset; a put _____ gives the buyer of the _____ the right to sell the underlying asset.

a. A Stake in the Outcome
b. A4e
c. AAAI
d. Option

27. In business and engineering, new _____ is the term used to describe the complete process of bringing a new product or service to market. There are two parallel paths involved in the NProduct development process: one involves the idea generation, product design, and detail engineering; the other involves market research and marketing analysis. Companies typically see new _____ as the first stage in generating and commercializing new products within the overall strategic process of product life cycle management used to maintain or grow their market share.

a. 28-hour day
b. 33 Strategies of War
c. 1990 Clean Air Act
d. Product development

Chapter 6. Strategic Management: How Star Managers Realize a Grand Design

1. _____ can be regarded as an outcome of mental processes (cognitive process) leading to the selection of a course of action among several alternatives. Every _____ process produces a final choice. The output can be an action or an opinion of choice.

    a. 33 Strategies of War
    b. 1990 Clean Air Act
    c. 28-hour day
    d. Decision making

2. A _____ is a brief written statement of the purpose of a company or organization. Ideally, a _____ guides the actions of the organization, spells out its overall goal, provides a sense of direction, and guides decision making for all levels of management.

_____s often contain the following:

- Purpose and aim of the organization
- The organization's primary stakeholders: clients, stockholders, etc.
- Responsibilities of the organization toward these stakeholders
- Products and services offered

In developing a _____:

- Encourage as much input as feasible from employees, volunteers, and other stakeholders
- Publicize it broadly

The _____ can be used to resolve differences between business stakeholders. Stakeholders include: employees including managers and executives, stockholders, board of directors, customers, suppliers, distributors, creditors, governments (local, state, federal, etc.), unions, competitors, NGO's, and the general public.

    a. 1990 Clean Air Act
    b. 33 Strategies of War
    c. 28-hour day
    d. Mission statement

3. _____ is an organization's process of defining its strategy and making decisions on allocating its resources to pursue this strategy, including its capital and people. Various business analysis techniques can be used in _____, including SWOT analysis (Strengths, Weaknesses, Opportunities, and Threats) and PEST analysis (Political, Economic, Social, and Technological analysis) or STEER analysis involving Socio-cultural, Technological, Economic, Ecological, and Regulatory factors and EPISTEL (Environment, Political, Informatic, Social, Technological, Economic and Legal)

_____ is the formal consideration of an organization's future course. All _____ deals with at least one of three key questions:

1. 'What do we do?'
2. 'For whom do we do it?'
3. 'How do we excel?'

In business _____, the third question is better phrased 'How can we beat or avoid competition?'. (Bradford and Duncan, page 1.)

a. 33 Strategies of War
c. 1990 Clean Air Act
b. Strategic planning
d. 28-hour day

4. A _____ is a formal statement of a set of business goals, the reasons why they are believed attainable, and the plan for reaching those goals. It may also contain background information about the organization or team attempting to reach those goals.

The business goals may be defined for for-profit or for non-profit organizations.

a. Crisis management
c. Time management
b. Distributed management
d. Business plan

5. _____ according to Onuoha (2007) is the practice of starting new organizations or revitalizing mature organizations, particularly new businesses generally in response to identified opportunities. _____ is often a difficult undertaking, as a vast majority of new businesses fail. Entrepreneurial activities are substantially different depending on the type of organization that is being started.

a. Entrepreneurship
c. A4e
b. AAAI
d. A Stake in the Outcome

6. _____ is one of the managerial functions like planning, organizing, staffing and directing. It is an important function because it helps to check the errors and to take the corrective action so that deviation from standards are minimized and stated goals of the organization are achieved in desired manner. According to modern concepts, _____ is a foreseeing action whereas earlier concept of _____ was used only when errors were detected. _____ in management means setting standards, measuring actual performance and taking corrective action.

a. Turnover
c. Control
b. Decision tree pruning
d. Schedule of reinforcement

7. _____ is a group creativity technique designed to generate a large number of ideas for the solution of a problem. The method was first popularized in the late 1930s by Alex Faickney Osborn in a book called Applied Imagination. Osborn proposed that groups could double their creative output with _____.

a. Abraham Harold Maslow
c. Affiliation
b. Brainstorming
d. Adam Smith

8. _____ is, in very basic words, a position a firm occupies against its competitors.

According to Michael Porter, the three methods for creating a sustainable _____ are through:

1. Cost leadership

2. Differentiation

3. Focus (economics)

a. 28-hour day
c. Theory Z
b. 1990 Clean Air Act
d. Competitive advantage

Chapter 6. Strategic Management: How Star Managers Realize a Grand Design

9. In marketing, _____ has come to mean the process by which marketers try to create an image or identity in the minds of their target market for its product, brand, or organization. It is the 'relative competitive comparison' their product occupies in a given market as perceived by the target market.

Re-_____ involves changing the identity of a product, relative to the identity of competing products, in the collective minds of the target market.

 a. PEST analysis
 c. Customer analytics
 b. Positioning
 d. Context analysis

10. Competitive advantage is, in very basic words, a position a firm occupies against its competitors.

According to Michael Porter, the three methods for creating a _____ are through:

1. Cost leadership - Cost advantage occurs when a firm delivers the same services as its competitors but at a lower cost;

2.

 a. Sustainable competitive advantage
 c. 28-hour day
 b. 1990 Clean Air Act
 d. Theory Z

11. _____ consists of the sale of goods or merchandise from a fixed location, such as a department store, boutique or kiosk in small or individual lots for direct consumption by the purchaser. _____ may include subordinated services, such as delivery. Purchasers may be individuals or businesses.
 a. 28-hour day
 c. 1990 Clean Air Act
 b. Planogram
 d. Retailing

12. A _____ is a process in which a potential employee is evaluated by an employer for prospective employment in their company, organization and was established in the late 16th century.

A _____ typically precedes the hiring decision, and is used to evaluate the candidate. The interview is usually preceded by the evaluation of submitted résumés from interested candidates, then selecting a small number of candidates for interviews.

 a. Payrolling
 c. Supported employment
 b. Split shift
 d. Job interview

13. _____ in its literal sense is the process of transformation of local or regional phenomena into global ones. It can be described as a process by which the people of the world are unified into a single society and function together.

This process is a combination of economic, technological, sociocultural and political forces.

Chapter 6. Strategic Management: How Star Managers Realize a Grand Design

    a. Cost Management

    c. Histogram

    b. Collaborative Planning, Forecasting and Replenishment

    d. Globalization

14. _____ is a structured approach to transitioning individuals, teams, and organizations from a current state to a desired future state. The current definition of _____ includes both organizational _____ processes and individual _____ models, which together are used to manage the people side of change.

A number of models are available for understanding the transitioning of individuals through the phases of _____ and strengthening organizational development initiative in both government and corporate sectors.

    a. 33 Strategies of War

    c. 28-hour day

    b. Change management

    d. 1990 Clean Air Act

15. _____ is the process by which an organization deals with any major unpredictable event that threatens to harm the organization, its stakeholders, or the general public. Three elements are common to most definitions of crisis: (a) a threat to the organization, (b) the element of surprise, and (c) a short decision time.

Whereas risk management involves assessing potential threats and finding the best ways to avoid those threats, _____ involves dealing with the disasters after they have occurred.

    a. Crisis management

    c. C-A-K-E

    b. Business value

    d. Capability management

16. _____ is the act by an employer of terminating employment. Though such a decision can be made by an employer for a variety of reasons, ranging from an economic downturn to performance-related problems on the part of the employee, being fired has a strong stigma in many cultures. To be fired, as opposed to quitting voluntarily (or being laid off), is often perceived as being the employee's fault, and is therefore considered to be disgraceful and a sign of failure.

    a. Termination of employment

    c. Firing

    b. Severance package

    d. Layoff

17. In a human resources context, _____ or labor _____ is the rate at which an employer gains and loses employees. Simple ways to describe it are 'how long employees tend to stay' or 'the rate of traffic through the revolving door.' _____ is measured for individual companies and for their industry as a whole. If an employer is said to have a high _____ relative to its competitors, it means that employees of that company have a shorter average tenure than those of other companies in the same industry.

    a. Ten year occupational employment projection

    c. Continuous

    b. Career portfolios

    d. Turnover

18. A _____ is a change implemented to address a weakness identified in a management system. Normally _____s are implemented in response to a customer complaint, abnormal levels of internal nonconformity, nonconformities identified during an internal audit or adverse or unstable trends in product and process monitoring such as would be identified by SPC.

The process of determining a _____ requires identification of actions that can be taken to prevent or mitigate the weakness.

Chapter 6. Strategic Management: How Star Managers Realize a Grand Design

a. 28-hour day
b. 1990 Clean Air Act
c. Zero defects
d. Corrective action

19. _____ describes the situation when output from (or information about the result of) an event or phenomenon in the past will influence the same event/phenomenon in the present or future. When an event is part of a chain of cause-and-effect that forms a circuit or loop, then the event is said to 'feed back' into itself.

_____ is also a synonym for:

- _____ signal; the information about the initial event that is the basis for subsequent modification of the event.
- _____ loop; the causal path that leads from the initial generation of the _____ signal to the subsequent modification of the event.

_____ is a mechanism, process or signal that is looped back to control a system within itself. Such a loop is called a _____ loop.

a. Feedback loop
b. Positive feedback
c. 1990 Clean Air Act
d. Feedback

20. _____ is a process of gathering, analyzing, and dispensing information for tactical or strategic purposes. The _____ process entails obtaining both factual and subjective information on the business environments in which a company is operating or considering entering.

There are three ways of scanning the business environment:

- Ad-hoc scanning - Short term, infrequent examinations usually initiated by a crisis
- Regular scanning - Studies done on a regular schedule (say, once a year)
- Continuous scanning(also called continuous learning) - continuous structured data collection and processing on a broad range of environmental factors

Most commentators feel that in today's turbulent business environment the best scanning method available is continuous scanning. This allows the firm to :

-act quickly-take advantage of opportunities before competitors do-respond to environmental threats before significant damage is done

a. AAAI
b. A4e
c. Environmental scanning
d. A Stake in the Outcome

21. _____ is a strategic planning method used to evaluate the Strengths, Weaknesses, Opportunities, and Threats involved in a project or in a business venture. It involves specifying the objective of the business venture or project and identifying the internal and external factors that are favorable and unfavorable to achieving that objective. The technique is credited to Albert Humphrey, who led a convention at Stanford University in the 1960s and 1970s using data from Fortune 500 companies.

Chapter 6. Strategic Management: How Star Managers Realize a Grand Design

    a. Marketing
    c. Market share
    b. Corporate image
    d. SWOT analysis

22. _____ is the process of estimation in unknown situations. Prediction is a similar, but more general term. Both can refer to estimation of time series, cross-sectional or longitudinal data.
    a. 1990 Clean Air Act
    b. 33 Strategies of War
    c. Forecasting
    d. 28-hour day

23. _____ is a strategic planning method that some organizations use to make flexible long-term plans. It is in large part an adaptation and generalization of classic methods used by military intelligence.

The original method was that a group of analysts would generate simulation games for policy makers. In business applications, the emphasis on gaming the behavior of opponents was reduced (shifting more toward a game against nature). At Royal Dutch/Shell for example, _____ was viewed as changing mindsets about the exogenous part of the world, prior to formulating specific strategies.

    a. Scenario planning
    c. Retroactive overtime
    b. Labour productivity
    d. Time and attendance

24. The term '_____' refers to the concept of collecting information and attempting to spot a pattern in the information. In some fields of study, the term '_____' has more formally-defined meanings.

In project management _____ is a mathematical technique that uses historical results to predict future outcome.

    a. Least squares
    c. Stepwise regression
    b. Trend analysis
    d. Regression analysis

25. A _____ is a name or trademark connected with a product or producer. _____s have become increasingly important components of culture and the economy, now being described as 'cultural accessories and personal philosophies'.

Some people distinguish the psychological aspect of a _____ from the experiential aspect.

    a. Brand loyalty
    c. Brand extension
    b. Brand awareness
    d. Brand

26. _____ is the strategic and coherent approach to the management of an organisation's most valued assets - the people working there who individually and collectively contribute to the achievement of the objectives of the business. The terms '_____' and 'human resources' (HR) have largely replaced the term 'personnel management' as a description of the processes involved in managing people in organizations. In simple sense, _____ means employing people, developing their resources, utilizing, maintaining and compensating their services in tune with the job and organizational requirement.
    a. Progressive discipline
    c. Human resource management
    b. Job knowledge
    d. Revolving door syndrome

27. A _____ is a type of business entity in which partners (owners) share with each other the profits or losses of the business. _____s are often favored over corporations for taxation purposes, as the _____ structure does not generally incur a tax on profits before it is distributed to the partners (i.e. there is no dividend tax levied.) However, depending on the _____ structure and the jurisdiction in which it operates, owners of a _____ may be exposed to greater personal liability than they would as shareholders of a corporation.

   a. Federal Employers Liability Act
   c. Due process
   b. Mediation
   d. Partnership

28. _____ is a method by which the job performance of an employee is evaluated _____ is a part of career development.

_____s are regular reviews of employee performance within organizations

Generally, the aims of a _____ are to:

- Give feedback on performance to employees.
- Identify employee training needs.
- Document criteria used to allocate organizational rewards.
- Form a basis for personnel decisions: salary increases, promotions, disciplinary actions, etc.
- Provide the opportunity for organizational diagnosis and development.
- Facilitate communication between employee and administraton
- Validate selection techniques and human resource policies to meet federal Equal Employment Opportunity requirements.

A common approach to assessing performance is to use a numerical or scalar rating system whereby managers are asked to score an individual against a number of objectives/attributes. In some companies, employees receive assessments from their manager, peers, subordinates and customers while also performing a self assessment.

   a. Human resource management
   c. Personnel management
   b. Progressive discipline
   d. Performance appraisal

29. _____ is a concept related to the relative abilities of parties in a situation to exert influence over each other. If both parties are on an equal footing in a debate, then they will have equal _____, such as in a perfectly competitive market, or between an evenly matched monopoly and monopsony.

There are a number of fields where the concept of _____ has proven crucial to coherent analysis: game theory, labour economics, collective bargaining arrangements, diplomatic negotiations, settlement of litigation, the price of insurance, and any negotiation in general.

   a. Bargaining power
   c. Trade credit
   b. 1990 Clean Air Act
   d. Buy-sell agreement

Chapter 6. Strategic Management: How Star Managers Realize a Grand Design

30. _____, commonly known as e-commerce, consists of the buying and selling of products or services over electronic systems such as the Internet and other computer networks. The amount of trade conducted electronically has grown extraordinarily with widespread Internet usage. The use of commerce is conducted in this way, spurring and drawing on innovations in electronic funds transfer, supply chain management, Internet marketing, online transaction processing, electronic data interchange (EDI), inventory management systems, and automated data collection systems.
    a. A Stake in the Outcome
    b. A4e
    c. Electronic Commerce
    d. Online shopping

31. _____ is subcontracting a process, such as product design or manufacturing, to a third-party company. The decision to outsource is often made in the interest of lowering cost or making better use of time and energy costs, redirecting or conserving energy directed at the competencies of a particular business, or to make more efficient use of land, labor, capital, (information) technology and resources. _____ became part of the business lexicon during the 1980s.
    a. Outsourcing
    b. Operant conditioning
    c. Opinion leadership
    d. Unemployment insurance

32. _____ Management is the succession of strategies used by management as a product goes through its _____. The conditions in which a product is sold changes over time and must be managed as it moves through its succession of stages.

The _____ goes through many phases, involves many professional disciplines, and requires many skills, tools and processes.

    a. Job hunting
    b. Strategic Alliance
    c. Golden handshake
    d. Product life cycle

33. In economics, business, retail, and accounting, a _____ is the value of money that has been used up to produce something, and hence is not available for use anymore. In economics, a _____ is an alternative that is given up as a result of a decision. In business, the _____ may be one of acquisition, in which case the amount of money expended to acquire it is counted as _____.
    a. Fixed costs
    b. Cost allocation
    c. Cost overrun
    d. Cost

34. In decision theory and estimation theory, the _____ of an estimator, $\hat{\theta}$, of an unknown parameter of the distribution, θ, is the expected value of the loss function

$$R(\theta, \hat{\theta}) = \mathbb{E}_\theta L(\theta, \hat{\theta}) = \int L(\theta, \hat{\theta})\, dP_\theta.$$

- For a scalar parameter θ and a quadratic loss function,

$$L(\theta, \hat{\theta}) = (\theta - \hat{\theta})^2$$

the _____ function becomes the mean squared error of the estimate,

$$R(\theta, \hat{\theta}) = E_\theta (\theta - \hat{\theta})^2$$

- In density estimation, the unknown parameter is probability density itself. The loss function is typically chosen to be a norm in an appropriate function space. For example, for L^2 norm,

$$L(f, \hat{f}) = \|f - \hat{f}\|_2^2$$

the _____ function becomes the mean integrated squared error

$$R(f, \hat{f}) = E\|f - \hat{f}\|^2$$

a. Risk
c. Linear model

b. Financial modeling
d. Risk aversion

35. A broad definition of _____ is the action of gathering, analyzing, and distributing information about products, customers, competitors and any aspect of the environment needed to support executives and managers in making strategic decisions for an organization.

Key points of this definitions:

1. _____ is an ethical and legal business practice. (This is important as _____ professionals emphasize that the discipline is not the same as industrial espionage which is both unethical and usually illegal.)
2. The focus is on the external business environment.
3. There is a process involved in gathering information, converting it into intelligence and then utilizing this in business decision making. _____ professionals emphasize that if the intelligence gathered is not usable (or actionable) then it is not intelligence.

Chapter 6. Strategic Management: How Star Managers Realize a Grand Design 61

A more focused definition of _____ regards it as the organizational function responsible for the early identification of risks and opportunities in the market before they become obvious. Experts also call this process the early signal analysis. This definition focuses attention on the difference between dissemination of widely available factual information (such as market statistics, financial reports, newspaper clippings) performed by functions such as libraries and information centers, and _____ which is a perspective on developments and events aimed at yielding a competitive edge.

   a. 28-hour day
   b. Competitive intelligence
   c. Competitor or Competitive Intelligence
   d. 1990 Clean Air Act

36. The U.S. _____ is an independent agency of the United States government which holds primary responsibility for enforcing the federal securities laws and regulating the securities industry, the nation's stock and options exchanges, and other electronic securities markets. The SEC was created by section 4 of the Securities Exchange Act of 1934 (now codified as 15 U.S.C. Â§ 78d and commonly referred to as the 1934 Act.)

   a. 33 Strategies of War
   b. 28-hour day
   c. 1990 Clean Air Act
   d. Securities and Exchange Commission

37. _____ is the term used to describe a situation where different entities cooperate advantageously for a final outcome. Simply defined, it means that the whole is greater than the sum of the individual parts. Although the whole will be greater than each individual part, this is not the concept of _____.

   a. 33 Strategies of War
   b. 28-hour day
   c. 1990 Clean Air Act
   d. Synergy

38. The _____ captures an expanded spectrum of values and criteria for measuring organizational success: economic, ecological and social. With the ratification of the United Nations and ICLEI _____ standard for urban and community accounting in early 2007, this became the dominant approach to public sector full cost accounting. Similar UN standards apply to natural capital and human capital measurement to assist in measurements required by _____, e.g. the ecoBudget standard for reporting ecological footprint.

   a. 28-hour day
   b. 33 Strategies of War
   c. 1990 Clean Air Act
   d. Triple bottom line

39. In economics and sociology, an _____ is any factor (financial or non-financial) that enables or motivates a particular course of action, or counts as a reason for preferring one choice to the alternatives. It is an expectation that encourages people to behave in a certain way. Since human beings are purposeful creatures, the study of _____ structures is central to the study of all economic activity (both in terms of individual decision-making and in terms of co-operation and competition within a larger institutional structure.)

   a. A Stake in the Outcome
   b. A4e
   c. AAAI
   d. Incentive

40. An _____ is a subset of strategic work plan. It describes short-term ways of achieving milestones and explains how, or what portion of, a strategic plan will be put into operation during a given operational period, in the case of commercial application, a fiscal year or another given budgetary term. An operational plan is the basis for, and justification of an annual operating budget request.

a. A4e
b. A Stake in the Outcome
c. AAAI
d. Operational planning

41. _____ is an idea in the field of Organizational studies and management which describes the psychology, attitudes, experiences, beliefs and Values (personal and cultural values) of an organization. It has been defined as 'the specific collection of values and norms that are shared by people and groups in an organization and that control the way they interact with each other and with stakeholders outside the organization.'

This definition continues to explain organizational values also known as 'beliefs and ideas about what kinds of goals members of an organization should pursue and ideas about the appropriate kinds or standards of behavior organizational members should use to achieve these goals. From organizational values develop organizational norms, guidelines or expectations that prescribe appropriate kinds of behavior by employees in particular situations and control the behavior of organizational members towards one another.'

_____ is not the same as corporate culture.

a. Organizational development
b. Union shop
c. Organizational effectiveness
d. Organizational culture

42. _____ is a term defined by the Oxford English Dictionary as an individual's 'course or progress through life '. It is usually considered to pertain to remunerative work (and sometimes also formal education.)

The etymology of the term is somewhat ironic in that it comes from the Latin word carrera, which means race .

a. Career
b. Career planning
c. Spatial mismatch
d. Nursing shortage

43. The phrase _____ refers to the aspect of corporate strategy, corporate finance and management dealing with the buying, selling and combining of different companies that can aid, finance, or help a growing company in a given industry grow rapidly without having to create another business entity.

An acquisition, also known as a takeover or a buyout, is the buying of one company (the 'target') by another. An acquisition may be friendly or hostile.

a. 33 Strategies of War
b. 1990 Clean Air Act
c. Mergers and acquisitions
d. 28-hour day

44. The phrase mergers and _____s refers to the aspect of corporate strategy, corporate finance and management dealing with the buying, selling and combining of different companies that can aid, finance, or help a growing company in a given industry grow rapidly without having to create another business entity.

An _____, also known as a takeover or a buyout, is the buying of one company (the 'target') by another. An _____ may be friendly or hostile.

a. A4e
b. AAAI
c. A Stake in the Outcome
d. Acquisition

Chapter 7. Individual & Group Decision Making: How Managers Make Things Happen

1. _____ can be regarded as an outcome of mental processes (cognitive process) leading to the selection of a course of action among several alternatives. Every _____ process produces a final choice. The output can be an action or an opinion of choice.
   a. 33 Strategies of War
   b. 1990 Clean Air Act
   c. Decision making
   d. 28-hour day

2. _____ is one of the managerial functions like planning, organizing, staffing and directing. It is an important function because it helps to check the errors and to take the corrective action so that deviation from standards are minimized and stated goals of the organization are achieved in desired manner. According to modern concepts, _____ is a foreseeing action whereas earlier concept of _____ was used only when errors were detected. _____ in management means setting standards, measuring actual performance and taking corrective action.
   a. Control
   b. Turnover
   c. Schedule of reinforcement
   d. Decision tree pruning

3. In decision theory and estimation theory, the _____ of an estimator, $\hat{\theta}$, of an unknown parameter of the distribution, θ, is the expected value of the loss function

$$R(\theta, \hat{\theta}) = \mathbb{E}_\theta L(\theta, \hat{\theta}) = \int L(\theta, \hat{\theta})\, dP_\theta.$$

where dP_θ is a probability measure parametrized by θ.

- For a scalar parameter θ and a quadratic loss function,

$$L(\theta, \hat{\theta}) = (\theta - \hat{\theta})^2$$

the _____ function becomes the mean squared error of the estimate,

$$R(\theta, \hat{\theta}) = E_\theta(\theta - \hat{\theta})^2$$

- In density estimation, the unknown parameter is probability density itself. The loss function is typically chosen to be a norm in an appropriate function space. For example, for L^2 norm,

$$L(f, \hat{f}) = \|f - \hat{f}\|_2^2$$

the _____ function becomes the mean integrated squared error

$$R(f, \hat{f}) = E\|f - \hat{f}\|^2$$

   a. Risk aversion
   b. Linear model
   c. Risk
   d. Financial modeling

Chapter 7. Individual & Group Decision Making: How Managers Make Things Happen 65

4. Engineering _____ is the permissible limit of variation in

   1. a physical dimension,
   2. a measured value or physical property of a material, manufactured object, system, or service,
   3. other measured values (such as temperature, humidity, etc.)
   4. in engineering and safety, a physical distance or space (_____), as in a truck (lorry), train or boat under a bridge as well as a train in a tunnel

Dimensions, properties, or conditions may vary within certain practical limits without significantly affecting functioning of equipment or a process. _____s are specified to allow reasonable leeway for imperfections and inherent variability without compromising performance.

The _____ may be specified as a factor or percentage of the nominal value, a maximum deviation from a nominal value, an explicit range of allowed values, be specified by a note or published standard with this information, or be implied by the numeric accuracy of the nominal value. _____ can be symmetrical, as in 40±0.1, or asymmetrical, such as 40+0.2/−0.1.

   a. Quality assurance
   b. Root cause analysis
   c. Zero defects
   d. Tolerance

5. _____ is, in very basic words, a position a firm occupies against its competitors.

According to Michael Porter, the three methods for creating a sustainable _____ are through:

1. Cost leadership

2. Differentiation

3. Focus (economics)

   a. 28-hour day
   b. 1990 Clean Air Act
   c. Theory Z
   d. Competitive advantage

6. _____ is a method by which the job performance of an employee is evaluated _____ is a part of career development.

   _____s are regular reviews of employee performance within organizations

Chapter 7. Individual & Group Decision Making: How Managers Make Things Happen

Generally, the aims of a _____ are to:

- Give feedback on performance to employees.
- Identify employee training needs.
- Document criteria used to allocate organizational rewards.
- Form a basis for personnel decisions: salary increases, promotions, disciplinary actions, etc.
- Provide the opportunity for organizational diagnosis and development.
- Facilitate communication between employee and administraton
- Validate selection techniques and human resource policies to meet federal Equal Employment Opportunity requirements.

A common approach to assessing performance is to use a numerical or scalar rating system whereby managers are asked to score an individual against a number of objectives/attributes. In some companies, employees receive assessments from their manager, peers, subordinates and customers while also performing a self assessment.

a. Progressive discipline
b. Performance appraisal
c. Human resource management
d. Personnel management

7. _____. The objective of OD is to improve the organization's capacity to handle its internal and external functioning and relationships. This would include such things as improved interpersonal and group processes, more effective communication, enhanced ability to cope with organizational problems of all kinds, more effective decision processes, more appropriate leadership style, improved skill in dealing with destructive conflict, and higher levels of trust and cooperation among organizational members.

a. Organizational development
b. Industrial relations
c. Organizational structure
d. Improved Organizational Performance

8. _____ is the provision of service to customers before, during and after a purchase.

According to Turban et al. (2002), '_____ is a series of activities designed to enhance the level of customer satisfaction - that is, the feeling that a product or service has met the customer expectation.'

Its importance varies by product, industry and customer; defective or broken merchandise can be exchanged, often only with a receipt and within a specified time frame.

a. 1990 Clean Air Act
b. Service rate
c. 28-hour day
d. Customer service

9. In economics, business, retail, and accounting, a _____ is the value of money that has been used up to produce something, and hence is not available for use anymore. In economics, a _____ is an alternative that is given up as a result of a decision. In business, the _____ may be one of acquisition, in which case the amount of money expended to acquire it is counted as _____.

a. Fixed costs
b. Cost
c. Cost overrun
d. Cost allocation

Chapter 7. Individual & Group Decision Making: How Managers Make Things Happen

10. _____ is an advertisement in which a particular product specifically mentions a competitor by name for the express purpose of showing why the competitor is inferior to the product naming it.

This should not be confused with parody advertisements, where a fictional product is being advertised for the purpose of poking fun at the particular advertisement, nor should it be confused with the use of a coined brand name for the purpose of comparing the product without actually naming an actual competitor. ('Wikipedia tastes better and is less filling than the Encyclopedia Galactica.')

In the 1980s, during what has been referred to as the cola wars, soft-drink manufacturer Pepsi ran a series of advertisements where people, caught on hidden camera, in a blind taste test, chose Pepsi over rival Coca-Cola.

a. Comparative advertising
b. 28-hour day
c. 1990 Clean Air Act
d. 33 Strategies of War

11. The '_____' states that any purposeful action will produce some unintended consequences. A classic example is a bypass -- a road built to relieve traffic congestion on a congested road -- that attracts new development and with it more traffic, resulting in two congested streets instead of one.

This maxim is not a scientific law; it is more in line with Murphy's law as a warning against the hubristic belief that humans can fully control the world around them.

a. 33 Strategies of War
b. 1990 Clean Air Act
c. Law of Unintended Consequences
d. 28-hour day

12. _____ are outcomes that are not (or not limited to) the results originally intended in a particular situation. The unintended results may be foreseen or unforeseen, but they should be the logical or likely results of the action. For example, historians have speculated that if the Treaty of Versailles had not imposed such harsh conditions on Germany, World War II would not have occurred.

a. Unintended consequences
b. AAAI
c. A4e
d. A Stake in the Outcome

13. _____ of the learning curve effect and the closely related experience curve effect express the relationship between equations for experience and efficiency or between efficiency gains and investment in the effort. The experience of 'learning curves' was first observed by the 19th Century German psychologist Hermann Ebbinghaus according to the difficulty of memorizing varying numbers of verbal stimuli, and subsequent learning about the complex processes of learning are discussed in the

.

The rule used for representing the learning curve effect states that the more times a task has been performed, the less time will be required on each subsequent iteration.

a. Distribution
b. Models
c. Spatial Decision Support Systems
d. Point biserial correlation coefficient

Chapter 7. Individual & Group Decision Making: How Managers Make Things Happen

14. _____ is a concept based on the fact that rationality of individuals is limited by the information they have, the cognitive limitations of their minds, and the finite amount of time they have to make decisions. This contrasts with the concept of rationality as optimization. Another way to look at _____ is that, because decision-makers lack the ability and resources to arrive at the optimal solution, they instead apply their rationality only after having greatly simplified the choices available.
    a. Transferable utility
    b. Mixed strategy
    c. Bounded rationality
    d. Complete information

15. _____ describes how content an individual is with his or her job.

The happier people are within their job, the more satisfied they are said to be. _____ is not the same as motivation, although it is clearly linked.

    a. Human relations
    b. Job analysis
    c. Goal-setting theory
    d. Job satisfaction

16. _____ is the process of extracting hidden patterns from data. As more data is gathered, with the amount of data doubling every three years, _____ is becoming an increasingly important tool to transform this data into information. It is commonly used in a wide range of profiling practices, such as marketing, surveillance, fraud detection and scientific discovery.
    a. Decision tree learning
    b. 1990 Clean Air Act
    c. 28-hour day
    d. Data mining

17. _____ is the process by which a model is created or chosen to try to best predict the probability of an outcome. In many cases the model is chosen on the basis of detection theory to try to guess the probability of a signal given a set amount of input data, for example given an email determining how likely that it is spam.

Models can use one or more classifiers in trying to determine the probability of a set of data belonging to another set, say spam or 'ham'.

    a. Predictive modeling
    b. 33 Strategies of War
    c. 1990 Clean Air Act
    d. 28-hour day

18. A _____ is a decision support tool that uses a tree-like graph or model of decisions and their possible consequences, including chance event outcomes, resource costs, and utility. _____s are commonly used in operations research, specifically in decision analysis, to help identify a strategy most likely to reach a goal. Another use of _____s is as a descriptive means for calculating conditional probabilities.
    a. 1990 Clean Air Act
    b. 33 Strategies of War
    c. 28-hour day
    d. Decision tree

19. A mutual _____ or stockholder is an individual or company (including a corporation) that legally owns one or more shares of stock in a joint stock company. A company's _____s collectively own that company. Thus, the typical goal of such companies is to enhance _____ value.
    a. Free riding
    b. Stockholder
    c. 1990 Clean Air Act
    d. Shareholder

Chapter 7. Individual & Group Decision Making: How Managers Make Things Happen

20. _____ is a business buzz term, which implies that the ultimate measure of a company's success is to enrich shareholders. It became popular during the 1980s, and is particularly associated with former CEO of General Electric, Jack Welch. In March 2009, Welch openly turned his back on the concept, calling _____ 'the dumbest idea in the world'.
   a. Shareholder value
   b. Sweat equity
   c. Corporate finance
   d. Gross profit margin

21. An _____ is a situation that will often involve an apparent conflict between moral imperatives, in which to obey one would result in transgressing another. This is also called an ethical paradox since in moral philosophy, paradox plays a central role in ethics debates. For instance, an ethical admonition to 'love thy neighbour as thy self' is not always just in contrast with, but sometimes in contradiction to an armed neighbour actively trying to kill you: if he or she succeeds, you will not be able to love him or her.
   a. A Stake in the Outcome
   b. A4e
   c. AAAI
   d. Ethical dilemma

22. _____ is decision making in groups consisting of multiple members/entities. The challenge of group decision is deciding what action a group should take. There are various systems designed to solve this problem.
   a. Collaborative Planning, Forecasting and Replenishment
   b. Genbutsu
   c. Control of Substances Hazardous to Health Regulations 2002
   d. Groups decision making

23. _____ is a type of thought exhibited by group members who try to minimize conflict and reach consensus without critically testing, analyzing, and evaluating ideas. Individual creativity, uniqueness, and independent thinking are lost in the pursuit of group cohesiveness, as are the advantages of reasonable balance in choice and thought that might normally be obtained by making decisions as a group. During _____, members of the group avoid promoting viewpoints outside the comfort zone of consensus thinking.
   a. Diffusion of responsibility
   b. Self-report inventory
   c. Psychological statistics
   d. Groupthink

24. _____ is the strategic and coherent approach to the management of an organisation's most valued assets - the people working there who individually and collectively contribute to the achievement of the objectives of the business. The terms '_____' and 'human resources' (HR) have largely replaced the term 'personnel management' as a description of the processes involved in managing people in organizations. In simple sense, _____ means employing people, developing their resources, utilizing, maintaining and compensating their services in tune with the job and organizational requirement.
   a. Human resource management
   b. Progressive discipline
   c. Job knowledge
   d. Revolving door syndrome

25. In economics and sociology, an _____ is any factor (financial or non-financial) that enables or motivates a particular course of action, or counts as a reason for preferring one choice to the alternatives. It is an expectation that encourages people to behave in a certain way. Since human beings are purposeful creatures, the study of _____ structures is central to the study of all economic activity (both in terms of individual decision-making and in terms of co-operation and competition within a larger institutional structure.)
   a. AAAI
   b. A4e
   c. A Stake in the Outcome
   d. Incentive

Chapter 7. Individual & Group Decision Making: How Managers Make Things Happen

26. _____ is a group creativity technique designed to generate a large number of ideas for the solution of a problem. The method was first popularized in the late 1930s by Alex Faickney Osborn in a book called Applied Imagination. Osborn proposed that groups could double their creative output with _____.

   a. Adam Smith
   b. Affiliation
   c. Abraham Harold Maslow
   d. Brainstorming

27. 6-3-5 _____ is a group creativity technique used in marketing, advertising, design, writing and product development originally developed by Professor Bernd Rohrbach in 1968.

Based on the concept of Brainstorming, the aim of 6-3-5 _____ is to generate 108 new ideas in half an hour. In a similar way to brainstorming, it is not the quality of ideas that matters but the quantity.

The technique involves 6 participants who sit in a group and are supervised by a moderator. Each participant thinks up 3 ideas every 5 minutes. Participants are encouraged to draw on others' ideas for inspiration, thus stimulating the creative process. After 6 rounds in 30 minutes the group has thought up a total of 108 ideas.

   a. 1990 Clean Air Act
   b. 28-hour day
   c. 33 Strategies of War
   d. Brainwriting

28. In a human resources context, _____ or labor _____ is the rate at which an employer gains and loses employees. Simple ways to describe it are 'how long employees tend to stay' or 'the rate of traffic through the revolving door.' _____ is measured for individual companies and for their industry as a whole. If an employer is said to have a high _____ relative to its competitors, it means that employees of that company have a shorter average tenure than those of other companies in the same industry.

   a. Career portfolios
   b. Continuous
   c. Ten year occupational employment projection
   d. Turnover

29. _____ is an adjective for experience-based techniques that help in problem solving, learning and discovery. A _____ method is particularly used to rapidly come to a solution that is hoped to be close to the best possible answer, or 'optimal solution'. _____s are 'rules of thumb', educated guesses, intuitive judgments or simply common sense.

   a. 1990 Clean Air Act
   b. Heuristic
   c. Representativeness
   d. 28-hour day

30. In psychology and cognitive science, _____ is a tendency to search for or interpret new information in a way that confirms one's preconceptions and to irrationally avoid information and interpretations which contradict prior beliefs. _____ is a type of cognitive bias and represents an error of inductive inference, or as a form of selection bias toward confirmation of the hypothesis under study or disconfirmation of an alternative hypothesis.

_____ is of interest in the teaching of critical thinking, as the skill (of thinking critically) is misused if rigorous critical scrutiny is applied only to evidence challenging a preconceived idea but not to evidence supporting it.

   a. Self-serving bias
   b. Choice-supportive bias
   c. Cognitive biases
   d. Confirmation bias

Chapter 7. Individual & Group Decision Making: How Managers Make Things Happen

31. The _____ heuristic is a heuristic wherein people assume commonality between objects of similar appearance, or between an object and a group it appears to fit into. While often very useful in everyday life, it can also result in neglect of relevant base rates and other cognitive biases. The representative heuristic was first proposed by Amos Tversky and Daniel Kahneman.
    a. 28-hour day
    b. Representativeness
    c. Representativeness heuristic
    d. 1990 Clean Air Act

32. _____ was first described by Barry M. Staw in his 1976 paper, 'Knee deep in the big muddy: A study of escalating commitment to a chosen course of action'. More recently the term Sunk cost fallacy has been used to describe the phenomenon where people justify increased investment in a decision, based on the cumulative prior investment, despite new evidence suggesting that the decision was probably wrong. Such investment may include money , time, or -- in the case of military strategy -- human lives.
    a. Escalation of commitment
    b. A4e
    c. Open Options
    d. A Stake in the Outcome

33. _____ is a theory that describes decisions between alternatives that involve risk, i.e. alternatives with uncertain outcomes, where the probabilities are known. The model is descriptive: it tries to model real-life choices, rather than optimal decisions.

    _____ was developed by Daniel Kahneman, professor at Princeton University's Department of Psychology, and Amos Tversky in 1979 as a psychologically realistic alternative to expected utility theory.

    a. 1990 Clean Air Act
    b. Prospect theory
    c. Loss aversion
    d. Mental accounting

34. In game theory, an _____ is a set of moves or strategies taken by the players, or their payoffs resulting from the actions or strategies taken by all players. The two are complementary in that given knowledge of the set of strategies of all players, the final state of the game is known, as are any relevant payoffs. In a game where chance or a random event is involved, the _____ is not known from only the set of strategies, but is only realized when the random event(s) are realized.
    a. AAAI
    b. A Stake in the Outcome
    c. A4e
    d. Outcome

Chapter 8. Organizational Culture, Structure, & Design

1. _____ 'is the use of one's individual or assigned power within an employing organization for the purpose of obtaining advantages beyond one's legitimate authority. Those advantages may include access to tangible assets, or intangible benefits such as status or pseudo-authority that influences the behavior of others. Both individuals and groups may engage in _____.'

_____ differs from office gossip in that people participating in _____ do so with the objective of gaining advantage, whereas gossip can be a purely social activity.

    a. A Stake in the Outcome   b. A4e
    c. AAAI   d. Office politics

2. _____ is one of the managerial functions like planning, organizing, staffing and directing. It is an important function because it helps to check the errors and to take the corrective action so that deviation from standards are minimized and stated goals of the organization are achieved in desired manner. According to modern concepts, _____ is a foreseeing action whereas earlier concept of _____ was used only when errors were detected. _____ in management means setting standards, measuring actual performance and taking corrective action.

    a. Decision tree pruning   b. Schedule of reinforcement
    c. Turnover   d. Control

3. _____ is a type of organization being antonymous to bureaucracy. The term was first popularized in 1970 by Alvin Toffler, and has since become often used in the theory of management of organizations (particularly online organizations), further developed by academics such as Henry Mintzberg. Robert H. Waterman, Jr. defined _____ as 'any form of organization that cuts across normal bureaucratic lines to capture opportunities, solve problems, and get results'.

    a. A4e   b. A Stake in the Outcome
    c. AAAI   d. Adhocracy

4. _____ is an idea in the field of Organizational studies and management which describes the psychology, attitudes, experiences, beliefs and Values (personal and cultural values) of an organization. It has been defined as 'the specific collection of values and norms that are shared by people and groups in an organization and that control the way they interact with each other and with stakeholders outside the organization.'

This definition continues to explain organizational values also known as 'beliefs and ideas about what kinds of goals members of an organization should pursue and ideas about the appropriate kinds or standards of behavior organizational members should use to achieve these goals. From organizational values develop organizational norms, guidelines or expectations that prescribe appropriate kinds of behavior by employees in particular situations and control the behavior of organizational members towards one another.'

_____ is not the same as corporate culture.

    a. Organizational development   b. Organizational culture
    c. Union shop   d. Organizational effectiveness

5. The _____ is a form of reactivity whereby subjects improve an aspect of their behavior being experimentally measured simply in response to the fact that they are being studied, not in response to any particular experimental manipulation.

Chapter 8. Organizational Culture, Structure, & Design

The term was coined in 1955 by Henry A. Landsberger when analyzing older experiments from 1924-1932 at the Hawthorne Works (outside Chicago.) Hawthorne Works had commissioned a study to see if its workers would become more productive in higher or lower levels of light.

- a. 1990 Clean Air Act
- b. 28-hour day
- c. 33 Strategies of War
- d. Hawthorne effect

6. _____ is a term defined by the Oxford English Dictionary as an individual's 'course or progress through life '. It is usually considered to pertain to remunerative work (and sometimes also formal education.)

The etymology of the term is somewhat ironic in that it comes from the Latin word carrera, which means race .

- a. Nursing shortage
- b. Career planning
- c. Spatial mismatch
- d. Career

7. In economics and sociology, an _____ is any factor (financial or non-financial) that enables or motivates a particular course of action, or counts as a reason for preferring one choice to the alternatives. It is an expectation that encourages people to behave in a certain way. Since human beings are purposeful creatures, the study of _____ structures is central to the study of all economic activity (both in terms of individual decision-making and in terms of co-operation and competition within a larger institutional structure.)
- a. Incentive
- b. A4e
- c. A Stake in the Outcome
- d. AAAI

8. An _____ is a mostly hierarchical concept of subordination of entities that collaborate and contribute to serve one common aim.

Organizations are a variant of clustered entities. The structure of an organization is usually set up in many a styles, dependent on their objectives and ambience.

- a. Informal organization
- b. Organizational structure
- c. Open shop
- d. Organizational development

9. _____ is a method by which the job performance of an employee is evaluated _____ is a part of career development.

_____s are regular reviews of employee performance within organizations

Chapter 8. Organizational Culture, Structure, & Design

Generally, the aims of a _____ are to:

- Give feedback on performance to employees.
- Identify employee training needs.
- Document criteria used to allocate organizational rewards.
- Form a basis for personnel decisions: salary increases, promotions, disciplinary actions, etc.
- Provide the opportunity for organizational diagnosis and development.
- Facilitate communication between employee and administraton
- Validate selection techniques and human resource policies to meet federal Equal Employment Opportunity requirements.

A common approach to assessing performance is to use a numerical or scalar rating system whereby managers are asked to score an individual against a number of objectives/attributes. In some companies, employees receive assessments from their manager, peers, subordinates and customers while also performing a self assessment.

   a. Personnel management   b. Performance appraisal
   c. Progressive discipline   d. Human resource management

10. _____ is a recursive process where two or more people or organizations work together in an intersection of common goals -- for example, an intellectual endeavor that is creative in nature--by sharing knowledge, learning and building consensus. _____ does not require leadership and can sometimes bring better results through decentralization and egalitarianism. In particular, teams that work collaboratively can obtain greater resources, recognition and reward when facing competition for finite resources. _____ is also present in opposing goals exhibiting the notion of adversarial _____, though this is not a common case for using the term.

   a. 28-hour day   b. 1990 Clean Air Act
   c. Collectivism   d. Collaboration

11. An _____, or organogram(me)) is a diagram that shows the structure of an organization and the relationships and relative ranks of its parts and positions/jobs. The term is also used for similar diagrams, for example ones showing the different elements of a field of knowledge or a group of languages. The French Encyclopédie had one of the first _____s of knowledge in general.

   a. AAAI   b. A Stake in the Outcome
   c. Organizational chart   d. A4e

12. In a military context, the _____ is the line of authority and responsibility along which orders are passed within a military unit and between different units. The term is also used in a civilian management context describing comparable hierarchical structures of authority.

   a. French leave   b. 28-hour day
   c. 1990 Clean Air Act   d. Chain of command

13. There are two types of _____ relationships: formal and informal. Informal relationships develop on their own between partners. Formal _____, on the other hand, refers to assigned relationships, often associated with organizational _____ programs designed to promote employee development or to assist at-risk children and youth.

Chapter 8. Organizational Culture, Structure, & Design

a. Real Property Administrator
b. Fix it twice
c. Human resource management system
d. Mentoring

14. The _____ is a standardized, on-scene, all-hazard incident management concept. It is a management protocol originally designed for emergency management agencies in the United States which was later federalized there. It has since been adopted by agencies in other countries.

a. Incident Command Structure
b. A Stake in the Outcome
c. AAAI
d. A4e

15. _____ is a concept in ethics with several meanings. It is often used synonymously with such concepts as responsibility, answerability, enforcement, blameworthiness, liability and other terms associated with the expectation of account-giving. As an aspect of governance, it has been central to discussions related to problems in both the public and private (corporation) worlds.

a. A4e
b. Accountability
c. Usury
d. A Stake in the Outcome

16. In economics, _____ are business expenses that are not dependent on the activities of the business They tend to be time-related, such as salaries or rents being paid per month. This is in contrast to variable costs, which are volume-related (and are paid per quantity.)

In management accounting, _____ are defined as expenses that do not change in proportion to the activity of a business, within the relevant period or scale of production.

a. Fixed costs
b. Cost of quality
c. Transaction cost
d. Cost allocation

17. _____ (known as horizontal organization) refers to an organizational structure with few or no levels of intervening management between staff and managers. The idea is that well-trained workers will be more productive when they are more directly involved in the decision making process, rather than closely supervised by many layers of management.

This structure is generally possible only in smaller organizations or individual units within larger organizations.

a. 33 Strategies of War
b. 1990 Clean Air Act
c. Flat organization
d. 28-hour day

18. _____ is a term originating in military organization theory, but now used more commonly in business management, particularly human resource management. _____ refers to the number of subordinates a supervisor has.

In the hierarchical business organization of the past it was not uncommon to see average spans of 1 to 10 or even less. That is, one manager supervised ten employees on average.

a. Mentoring
b. Senior management
c. CIFMS
d. Span of control

19. In economics, business, retail, and accounting, a _____ is the value of money that has been used up to produce something, and hence is not available for use anymore. In economics, a _____ is an alternative that is given up as a result of a decision. In business, the _____ may be one of acquisition, in which case the amount of money expended to acquire it is counted as _____.
   a. Cost allocation
   b. Cost
   c. Cost overrun
   d. Fixed costs

20. _____ can be regarded as an outcome of mental processes (cognitive process) leading to the selection of a course of action among several alternatives. Every _____ process produces a final choice. The output can be an action or an opinion of choice.
   a. Decision making
   b. 28-hour day
   c. 33 Strategies of War
   d. 1990 Clean Air Act

21. A _____ is a group of employees from various functional areas of the organization - research, engineering, marketing, finance. human resources, and operations, for example - who are all focused on a specific objective and are responsible to work as a team to improve coordination and innovation across divisions and resolve mutual problems.
   a. Graduate recruitment
   b. Cross-functional team
   c. Sociotechnical systems
   d. Goal-setting theory

22. _____ is subcontracting a process, such as product design or manufacturing, to a third-party company. The decision to outsource is often made in the interest of lowering cost or making better use of time and energy costs, redirecting or conserving energy directed at the competencies of a particular business, or to make more efficient use of land, labor, capital, (information) technology and resources. _____ became part of the business lexicon during the 1980s.
   a. Unemployment insurance
   b. Opinion leadership
   c. Operant conditioning
   d. Outsourcing

23. A _____ is a contemporary apporach to organizational design. It is an organization that is not defined by, or limited to, the horizontal, vertical, or external boundaries imposed by a predefined structure. This term was coined by former GE chairman Jack Welch because he wanted to eliminate vertical and horizontal boundaries within GE and break down external barriers between the company and its customers and suppliers.
   a. Business Roundtable
   b. Chief risk officer
   c. Headquarters
   d. Boundaryless organization

24. _____ is a work methodology based on the parallelization of tasks (ie. concurrently.) It refers to an approach used in product development in which functions of design engineering, manufacturing engineering and other functions are integrated to reduce the elapsed time required to bring a new product to the market.
   a. Project management
   b. Work package
   c. Concurrent engineering
   d. Critical Chain Project Management

25. In economics, a _____ exists when a specific individual or enterprise has sufficient control over a particular product or service to determine significantly the terms on which other individuals shall have access to it. Monopolies are thus characterized by a lack of economic competition for the good or service that they provide and a lack of viable substitute goods. The verb 'monopolize' refers to the process by which a firm gains persistently greater market share than what is expected under perfect competition.

a. Monopoly
b. 28-hour day
c. 33 Strategies of War
d. 1990 Clean Air Act

26. In business and engineering, new _____ is the term used to describe the complete process of bringing a new product or service to market. There are two parallel paths involved in the NProduct development process: one involves the idea generation, product design, and detail engineering; the other involves market research and marketing analysis. Companies typically see new _____ as the first stage in generating and commercializing new products within the overall strategic process of product life cycle management used to maintain or grow their market share.
   a. 1990 Clean Air Act
   b. 28-hour day
   c. 33 Strategies of War
   d. Product development

27. A _____ is a process in which a potential employee is evaluated by an employer for prospective employment in their company, organization and was established in the late 16th century.

A _____ typically precedes the hiring decision, and is used to evaluate the candidate. The interview is usually preceded by the evaluation of submitted résumés from interested candidates, then selecting a small number of candidates for interviews.

   a. Supported employment
   b. Split shift
   c. Payrolling
   d. Job interview

28. _____ is something that a firm can do well and that meets the following three conditions:

Competencies are things that companys execute well across several business units or product sectors.

Firms usually have few competencies, but these are usually less liable to change rapidly.

   1. It provides consumer benefits
   2. It is not easy for competitors to imitate
   3. It can be leveraged widely to many products and markets.

A _____ can take various forms, including technical/subject matter know-how, a reliable process and/or close relationships with customers and suppliers (Mascarenhas et al. 1998.)

   a. Core competency
   b. Learning-by-doing
   c. Dominant Design
   d. NAIRU

29. _____, in microeconomics, are the cost advantages that a business obtains due to expansion. They are factors that cause a producer's average cost per unit to fall as scale is increased. _____ is a long run concept and refers to reductions in unit cost as the size of a facility, or scale, increases.
   a. A4e
   b. Economies of scope
   c. Economies of scale
   d. A Stake in the Outcome

30. _____ in its literal sense is the process of transformation of local or regional phenomena into global ones. It can be described as a process by which the people of the world are unified into a single society and function together.

This process is a combination of economic, technological, sociocultural and political forces.

a. Cost Management

b. Globalization

c. Histogram

d. Collaborative Planning, Forecasting and Replenishment

31. _____ is the life cycle of an organization from birth level to the termination.

There are five level/stages in any organization.

1. Birth
2. Growth
3. Maturity
4. Decline
5. Death

According to Richard L. Daft there are four stages in an _____.

The four stages are:

1. Entrepreneurial stage -> Crisis: Need for leadership
2. Collectivity stage -> Crisis: Need for delegation
3. Formalization stage -> Crisis: Too much red tape
4. Elaboration stage -> Crisis: Need for revitalization

(Richard L. Daft, Understanding the Theory and Design of Organizations, first edition 2007, ISBN 0-324-42271-7)

a. A Stake in the Outcome

b. Organizational life cycle

c. AAAI

d. A4e

Chapter 9. Human Resource Management: Getting the Right People for Managerial Success

1. _____ describes the situation when output from (or information about the result of) an event or phenomenon in the past will influence the same event/phenomenon in the present or future. When an event is part of a chain of cause-and-effect that forms a circuit or loop, then the event is said to 'feed back' into itself.

_____ is also a synonym for:

- _____ signal; the information about the initial event that is the basis for subsequent modification of the event.
- _____ loop; the causal path that leads from the initial generation of the _____ signal to the subsequent modification of the event.

_____ is a mechanism, process or signal that is looped back to control a system within itself. Such a loop is called a _____ loop.

a. Positive feedback
b. 1990 Clean Air Act
c. Feedback loop
d. Feedback

2. _____ is the strategic and coherent approach to the management of an organisation's most valued assets - the people working there who individually and collectively contribute to the achievement of the objectives of the business. The terms '_____' and 'human resources' (HR) have largely replaced the term 'personnel management' as a description of the processes involved in managing people in organizations. In simple sense, _____ means employing people, developing their resources, utilizing, maintaining and compensating their services in tune with the job and organizational requirement.

a. Job knowledge
b. Revolving door syndrome
c. Progressive discipline
d. Human resource management

3. _____ is a method by which the job performance of an employee is evaluated _____ is a part of career development.

_____s are regular reviews of employee performance within organizations

Generally, the aims of a _____ are to:

- Give feedback on performance to employees.
- Identify employee training needs.
- Document criteria used to allocate organizational rewards.
- Form a basis for personnel decisions: salary increases, promotions, disciplinary actions, etc.
- Provide the opportunity for organizational diagnosis and development.
- Facilitate communication between employee and administraton
- Validate selection techniques and human resource policies to meet federal Equal Employment Opportunity requirements.

A common approach to assessing performance is to use a numerical or scalar rating system whereby managers are asked to score an individual against a number of objectives/attributes. In some companies, employees receive assessments from their manager, peers, subordinates and customers while also performing a self assessment.

Chapter 9. Human Resource Management: Getting the Right People for Managerial Success

a. Performance appraisal
b. Human resource management
c. Personnel management
d. Progressive discipline

4. _____ refers to the stock of skills and knowledge embodied in the ability to perform labor so as to produce economic value. It is the skills and knowledge gained by a worker through education and experience. Many early economic theories refer to it simply as labor, one of three factors of production, and consider it to be a fungible resource -- homogeneous and easily interchangeable.

a. Productivity management
b. Market structure
c. Deflation
d. Human capital

5. _____ is an organization's process of defining its strategy and making decisions on allocating its resources to pursue this strategy, including its capital and people. Various business analysis techniques can be used in _____, including SWOT analysis (Strengths, Weaknesses, Opportunities, and Threats) and PEST analysis (Political, Economic, Social, and Technological analysis) or STEER analysis involving Socio-cultural, Technological, Economic, Ecological, and Regulatory factors and EPISTEL (Environment, Political, Informatic, Social, Technological, Economic and Legal)

_____ is the formal consideration of an organization's future course. All _____ deals with at least one of three key questions:

1. 'What do we do?'
2. 'For whom do we do it?'
3. 'How do we excel?'

In business _____, the third question is better phrased 'How can we beat or avoid competition?'. (Bradford and Duncan, page 1.)

a. 33 Strategies of War
b. 28-hour day
c. 1990 Clean Air Act
d. Strategic planning

6. _____ is an increasingly broadening term with which an organization, or other human system describes the combination of traditionally administrative personnel functions with acquisition and application of skills, knowledge and experience, Employee Relations and resource planning at various levels. The field draws upon concepts developed in Industrial/Organizational Psychology and System Theory. _____ has at least two related interpretations depending on context. The original usage derives from political economy and economics, where it was traditionally called labor, one of four factors of production although this perspective is changing as a function of new and ongoing research into more strategic approaches at national levels. This first usage is used more in terms of '_____ development', and can go beyond just organizations to the level of nations . The more traditional usage within corporations and businesses refers to the individuals within a firm or agency, and to the portion of the organization that deals with hiring, firing, training, and other personnel issues, typically referred to as `_____ management'.

a. Bradford Factor
b. Human resources
c. Human resource management
d. Progressive discipline

7. _____ refers to various methodologies for analyzing the requirements of a job.

Chapter 9. Human Resource Management: Getting the Right People for Managerial Success

The general purpose of _____ is to document the requirements of a job and the work performed. Job and task analysis is performed as a basis for later improvements, including: definition of a job domain; describing a job; developing performance appraisals, selection systems, promotion criteria, training needs assessment, and compensation plans.

- a. Work design
- b. Hersey-Blanchard situational theory
- c. Management process
- d. Job analysis

8. A _____ is a list of the general tasks and responsibilities of a position. Typically, it also includes to whom the position reports, specifications such as the qualifications needed by the person in the job, salary range for the position, etc. A _____ is usually developed by conducting a job analysis, which includes examining the tasks and sequences of tasks necessary to perform the job.

- a. Recruitment
- b. Recruitment advertising
- c. Job description
- d. Recruitment Process Insourcing

9. In organized labor, _____ is the method whereby workers organize together (usually in unions) to meet, converse, and negotiate upon the work conditions with their employers normally resulting in a written contract setting forth the wages, hours, and other conditions to be observed for a stipulated period. It is the practice in which union and company representatives meet to negotiate a new labor contract. In various national labor and employment law contexts, the term _____ takes on a more specific legal meaning. In a broad sense, however, it is the coming together of workers to negotiate their employment.

- a. Labour law
- b. Labor rights
- c. Paid time off
- d. Collective bargaining

10. _____ is a contract between two parties, one being the employer and the other being the employee. An employee may be defined as: 'A person in the service of another under any contract of hire, express or implied, oral or written, where the employer has the power or right to control and direct the employee in the material details of how the work is to be performed.' Black's Law Dictionary page 471 (5th ed. 1979.)

- a. Employment rate
- b. Employment
- c. Employment counsellor
- d. Exit interview

11. The term _____ was created by President Lyndon B. Johnson when he signed Executive Order 11246 on September 24, 1965, created to prohibit federal contractors from discriminating against employees on the basis of race, sex, creed, religion, color, or national origin. In more recent times, most employers have also added sexual orientation to the list of non-discrimination.

The Executive Order also required contractors to implement affirmative action plans to increase the participation of minorities and women in the workplace.

- a. A4e
- b. AAAI
- c. A Stake in the Outcome
- d. Equal Employment Opportunity

Chapter 9. Human Resource Management: Getting the Right People for Managerial Success

12. The U.S. _____ is a federal agency whose goal is ending employment discrimination. The _____ investigates discrimination complaints based on an individual's race, color, national origin, religion, sex, age, disability and retaliation for reporting and/or opposing a discriminatory practice. The Commission is also tasked with filing suits on behalf of alleged victim(s) of discrimination against employers and as an adjudicatory for claims of discrimination brought against federal agencies.
    a. ARCO
    b. Airbus Industrie
    c. Airbus SAS
    d. Equal Employment Opportunity Commission

13. The _____ of 1938 (_____, ch. 676, 52 Stat. 1060, June 25, 1938, 29 U.S.C. ch.8), also called the Wages and Hours Bill, is United States federal law that applies to employees engaged in interstate commerce or employed by an enterprise engaged in commerce or in the production of goods for commerce, unless the employer can claim an exemption from coverage. The _____ established a national minimum wage, guaranteed time and a half for overtime in certain jobs, and prohibited most employment of minors in 'oppressive child labor,' a term defined in the statute.
    a. Joint venture
    b. Board of directors
    c. Fair Labor Standards Act
    d. Family and Medical Leave Act of 1993

14. In economics and sociology, an _____ is any factor (financial or non-financial) that enables or motivates a particular course of action, or counts as a reason for preferring one choice to the alternatives. It is an expectation that encourages people to behave in a certain way. Since human beings are purposeful creatures, the study of _____ structures is central to the study of all economic activity (both in terms of individual decision-making and in terms of co-operation and competition within a larger institutional structure.)
    a. AAAI
    b. A4e
    c. A Stake in the Outcome
    d. Incentive

15. The field of _____ looks at the relationship between management and workers, particularly groups of workers represented by a union.

    _____ is an important factor in analyzing 'varieties of capitalism', such as neocorporatism, social democracy, and neoliberalism

    a. Industrial relations
    b. Organizational effectiveness
    c. Informal organization
    d. Overtime

16. _____ are conventions, treaties and recommendations designed to eliminate unjust and inhumane labour practices. The primary inernational agency charged with developing such standards is the International Labour Organization (ILO.) Established in 1919, the ILO advocates international standards as essential for the eradication of labour conditions involving 'injustice, hardship and privation'.
    a. International labour standards
    b. Airbus Industrie
    c. Airbus SAS
    d. Anaconda Copper

17. A _____ is the lowest hourly, daily or monthly wage that employers may legally pay to employees or workers. Equivalently, it is the lowest wage at which workers may sell their labor. Although _____ laws are in effect in a great many jurisdictions, there are differences of opinion about the benefits and drawbacks of a _____.
    a. Value added
    b. Deregulation
    c. Minimum wage
    d. Rehn-Meidner Model

Chapter 9. Human Resource Management: Getting the Right People for Managerial Success

18. _____ is a cross-disciplinary area concerned with protecting the safety, health and welfare of people engaged in work or employment. The goal of all _____ programs is to foster a work free safe environment. As a secondary effect, it may also protect co-workers, family members, employers, customers, suppliers, nearby communities, and other members of the public who are impacted by the workplace environment.

   a. AAAI
   b. Occupational Safety and Health
   c. A Stake in the Outcome
   d. A4e

19. The _____ is the primary federal law which governs occupational health and safety in the private sector and federal government in the United States. It was enacted by Congress in 1970 and was signed by President Richard Nixon on December 29, 1970. Its main goal is to ensure that employers provide employees with an environment free from recognized hazards, such as exposure to toxic chemicals, excessive noise levels, mechanical dangers, heat or cold stress, or unsanitary conditions.

   a. Unemployment Action Center
   b. Unemployment and Farm Relief Act
   c. United States Department of Justice
   d. Occupational Safety and Health Act

20. A _____ is a compensation, usually financial, received by a worker in exchange for their labor.

Compensation in terms of _____s is given to worker and compensation in terms of salary is given to employees. Compensation is a monetary benefits given to employees in returns of the services provided by them.

   a. Performance-related pay
   b. State Compensation Insurance Fund
   c. Profit-sharing agreement
   d. Wage

21. _____ is a category of management responsibility in places of employment.

To ensure the safety and health of workers, managers establish a focus on safety that can include elements such as:

- management leadership and commitment
- employee engagement
- accountability
- ensuring all task are carried out safely and effeintly
- safety programs, policies, and plans
- safety processes, procedures, and practices
- safety goals and objectives
- safety inspections for workplace hazards
- safety program audits
- safety tracking ' metrics
- hazard identification and control
- safety committees to promote employee involvement
- safety education and training
- safety communications to maintain a high level of awareness on safety

Data from 2003

Chapter 9. Human Resource Management: Getting the Right People for Managerial Success

In most countries males comprise the vast majority of workplace fatalities. In the EU as a whole, 94% of death were of males.

The Bureau of Labor Statistics of the United States Department of Labor compiles information about workplace fatalities in the United States.

- a. 28-hour day
- b. 1990 Clean Air Act
- c. 33 Strategies of War
- d. Workplace safety

22. _____ is a concept in ethics with several meanings. It is often used synonymously with such concepts as responsibility, answerability, enforcement, blameworthiness, liability and other terms associated with the expectation of account-giving. As an aspect of governance, it has been central to discussions related to problems in both the public and private (corporation) worlds.
- a. A Stake in the Outcome
- b. A4e
- c. Usury
- d. Accountability

23. The _____ of 1967, Pub. L. No. 90-202, 81 Stat. 602 (Dec. 15, 1967), codified as Chapter 14 of Title 29 of the United States Code, 29 U.S.C. § 621 through 29 U.S.C. § 634 (ADEA), prohibits employment discrimination against persons 40 years of age or older in the United States). The law also sets standards for pensions and benefits provided by employers and requires that information about the needs of older workers be provided to the general public.
- a. Undue hardship
- b. Unemployment and Farm Relief Act
- c. Extra time
- d. Age Discrimination in Employment Act

24. _____ generally refers to a list of all planned expenses and revenues. It is a plan for saving and spending. A _____ is an important concept in microeconomics, which uses a _____ line to illustrate the trade-offs between two or more goods.
- a. 1990 Clean Air Act
- b. 33 Strategies of War
- c. 28-hour day
- d. Budget

25. The _____ of 1985 is a law passed by the U.S. Congress and signed by President Reagan that, among other things, mandates an insurance program giving some employees the ability to continue health insurance coverage after leaving employment. _____ includes amendments to the Employee Retirement Income Security Act of 1974 (ERISA.) The law deals with a great variety of subjects, such as tobacco price supports, railroads, private pension plans, disability insurance, and the postal service, but it is perhaps best known for Title X, which amends the Internal Revenue Code to deny income tax deductions to employers for contributions to a group health plan unless such plan meets certain continuing coverage requirements.
- a. 28-hour day
- b. 1990 Clean Air Act
- c. 33 Strategies of War
- d. Consolidated Omnibus Budget Reconciliation Act

26. _____ is one of the managerial functions like planning, organizing, staffing and directing. It is an important function because it helps to check the errors and to take the corrective action so that deviation from standards are minimized and stated goals of the organization are achieved in desired manner.According to modern concepts, _____ is a foreseeing action whereas earlier concept of _____ was used only when errors were detected. _____ in management means setting standards, measuring actual performance and taking corrective action.

Chapter 9. Human Resource Management: Getting the Right People for Managerial Success

a. Turnover
b. Decision tree pruning
c. Schedule of reinforcement
d. Control

27. The _____ 1970 is an Act of the United Kingdom Parliament which prohibits any less favourable treatment between men and women in terms of pay and conditions of employment. It came into force on 29 December 1975. The term pay is interpreted in a broad sense to include, on top of wages, things like holidays, pension rights, company perks and some kinds of bonuses.
    a. Equal Pay Act
    b. Australian labour law
    c. Oncale v. Sundowner Offshore Services
    d. Architectural Barriers Act of 1968

28. _____ occurs when expectant women are fired, not hired, or otherwise discriminated against due to their pregnancy or intention to become pregnant. Common forms of _____ include not being hired due to visible pregnancy or likelihood of becoming pregnant, being fired after informing an employer of one's pregnancy, being fired after maternity leave, and receiving a pay dock due to pregnancy. In the United States, since 1978, employers are legally bound to provide what insurance, leave pay, and additional support that would be bestowed upon any employee with medical leave or disability.
    a. 28-hour day
    b. 1990 Clean Air Act
    c. 33 Strategies of War
    d. Pregnancy Discrimination

29. _____ is the process of learning a new skill or trade, often in response to a change in the economic environment. Generally it reflects changes in profession choice rather than an 'upward' movement in the same field.

There is some controversy surrounding the use of _____ to offset economic changes caused by free trade and automation.

    a. Compliance Training
    b. Krauthammer
    c. Suspension training
    d. Retraining

30. The _____ of 2002 (Pub.L. 107-204, 116 Stat. 745, enacted July 30, 2002), also known as the Public Company Accounting Reform and Investor Protection Act of 2002 and commonly called Sarbanes-Oxley, Sarbox or SOX, is a United States federal law enacted on July 30, 2002, as a reaction to a number of major corporate and accounting scandals including those affecting Enron, Tyco International, Adelphia, Peregrine Systems and WorldCom.
    a. Fair Labor Standards Act
    b. Sarbanes-Oxley Act of 2002
    c. Letter of credit
    d. Sarbanes-Oxley Act

31.

The terms _____ and positive action refer to policies that take race, ethnicity, or gender into consideration in an attempt to promote equal opportunity. The focus of such policies ranges from employment and education to public contracting and health programs. The impetus towards _____ is twofold: to maximize diversity in all levels of society, along with its presumed benefits, and to redress perceived disadvantages due to overt, institutional, or involuntary discrimination.

    a. Adam Smith
    b. Affiliation
    c. Abraham Harold Maslow
    d. Affirmative action

Chapter 9. Human Resource Management: Getting the Right People for Managerial Success

32. The _____ of 1990 (ADA) is the short title of United States (Pub.L. 101-336, 104 Stat. 327, enacted July 26, 1990), codified at 42 U.S.C. § 12101 et seq. It was signed into law on July 26, 1990, by President George H. W. Bush, and later amended with changes effective January 1, 2009. The ADA is a wide-ranging civil rights law that prohibits, under certain circumstances, discrimination based on disability. It affords similar protections against discrimination to Americans with disabilities as the Civil Rights Act of 1964,

a. Employment discrimination
b. Americans with Disabilities Act
c. Australian labour law
d. Equal Pay Act of 1963

33. _____ indicates a more-or-less equal exchange or substitution of goods or services. English speakers often use the term to mean 'a favour for a favour' and the phrases with almost identical meaning include: 'what for what,' 'give and take,' 'tit for tat', 'this for that', and 'you scratch my back, and I'll scratch yours'.

In legal usage, _____ indicates that an item or a service has been traded in return for something of value, usually when the propriety or equity of the transaction is in question.

a. 28-hour day
b. 1990 Clean Air Act
c. 33 Strategies of War
d. Quid pro quo

34. _____ is unwelcome harassment of a sexual nature, or based upon the receiving party's sex or gender. In some contexts or circumstances, _____ may be illegal. It includes a range of behavior from seemingly mild transgressions and annoyances to actual sexual abuse or sexual assault.

a. 28-hour day
b. Hypernorms
c. 1990 Clean Air Act
d. Sexual harassment

35. _____ refers to the process of screening, and selecting qualified people for a job at an organization or firm mid- and large-size organizations and companies often retain professional recruiters or outsource some of the process to _____ agencies. External _____ is the process of attracting and selecting employees from outside the organization.

The _____ industry has four main types of agencies: employment agencies, _____ websites and job search engines, 'headhunters' for executive and professional _____, and in-house _____.

a. Recruitment Process Outsourcing
b. Referral recruitment
c. Labour hire
d. Recruitment

36. _____ are a method of interviews where questions can be changed or adapted to meet the respondent's intelligence, understanding or belief. Unlike a structured interview they do not offer a limited, pre-set range of answers for a respondent to choose, but instead advocate listening to how each individual person responds to the question.

The method to gather information using this technique is fairly limited, for example most surveys that are carried out via telephone or even in person tend to follow a structured method.

a. AAAI
b. A4e
c. A Stake in the Outcome
d. Unstructured interviews

Chapter 9. Human Resource Management: Getting the Right People for Managerial Success

37. _____ is an idea in the field of Organizational studies and management which describes the psychology, attitudes, experiences, beliefs and Values (personal and cultural values) of an organization. It has been defined as 'the specific collection of values and norms that are shared by people and groups in an organization and that control the way they interact with each other and with stakeholders outside the organization.'

This definition continues to explain organizational values also known as 'beliefs and ideas about what kinds of goals members of an organization should pursue and ideas about the appropriate kinds or standards of behavior organizational members should use to achieve these goals. From organizational values develop organizational norms, guidelines or expectations that prescribe appropriate kinds of behavior by employees in particular situations and control the behavior of organizational members towards one another.'

_____ is not the same as corporate culture.

a. Organizational development
b. Union shop
c. Organizational effectiveness
d. Organizational culture

38. A _____ is a quantitative research method commonly employed in survey research. The aim of this approach is to ensure that each interviewee is presented with exactly the same questions in the same order. This ensures that answers can be reliably aggregated and that comparisons can be made with confidence between sample subgroups or between different survey periods.

a. Questionnaire
b. Structured interview
c. Questionnaire construction
d. Mystery shoppers

39. The _____ assessment is a psychometric questionnaire designed to measure psychological preferences in how people perceive the world and make decisions.[1] These preferences were extrapolated from the typological theories originated by Carl Gustav Jung, as published in his 1921 book Psychological Types. The original developers of the personality inventory were Katharine Cook Briggs and her daughter, Isabel Briggs Myers. They began creating the indicator during World War II, believing that a knowledge of personality preferences would help women who were entering the industrial workforce for the first time identify the sort of war-time jobs where they would be 'most comfortable and effective'.[xiii] The initial questionnaire grew into the _____, which was first published in 1962.

a. 1990 Clean Air Act
b. 33 Strategies of War
c. Myers-Briggs Type Indicator
d. 28-hour day

40. Performance Testing covers a broad range of engineering or functional evaluations where a material, product, system emphasis is on the final measurable performance characteristics.

Performance testing can refer to the assessment of the performance of a human examinee. For example, a behind-the-wheel driving test is a _____ of whether a person is able to perform the functions of a competent driver of an automobile.

a. 28-hour day
b. Reverse engineering
c. Performance test
d. 1990 Clean Air Act

Chapter 9. Human Resource Management: Getting the Right People for Managerial Success

41. _____, e-commuting, e-work, telework, working from home (WFH), or working at home (WAH) is a work arrangement in which employees enjoy flexibility in working location and hours. In other words, the daily commute to a central place of work is replaced by telecommunication links. Many work from home, while others, occasionally also referred to as nomad workers or web commuters utilize mobile telecommunications technology to work from coffee shops or myriad other locations.
   a. 28-hour day
   b. Telecommuting
   c. 1990 Clean Air Act
   d. 33 Strategies of War

42. The term _____ in logic applies to arguments or statements.

An argument is valid if and only if the truth of its premises entails the truth of its conclusion, it would be self-contradictory to affirm the premises and deny the conclusion. The corresponding conditional of a valid argument is a logical truth and the negation of its corresponding conditional is a contradiction.

   a. Simplification
   b. Validity
   c. Fuzzy logic
   d. 1990 Clean Air Act

43. In the field of human resource management, _____ is the field concerned with organizational activity aimed at bettering the performance of individuals and groups in organizational settings. It has been known by several names, including employee development, human resource development, and learning and development.

Harrison observes that the name was endlessly debated by the Chartered Institute of Personnel and Development during its review of professional standards in 1999/2000.

   a. Revolving door syndrome
   b. Person specification
   c. Performance appraisal
   d. Training and development

44. _____ is an all encompassing term within a broad spectrum of post-secondary learning activities and programs. The term is used mainly in the United States. Recognized forms of post-secondary learning activities within the domain include: degree credit courses by non-traditional students, non-degree career training, workforce training, formal personal enrichment courses (both on-campus and online) self-directed learning (such as through Internet interest groups, clubs or personal research activities) and experiential learning as applied to problem solving.
   a. 28-hour day
   b. 1990 Clean Air Act
   c. 33 Strategies of War
   d. Continuing education

45. _____ is a forward looking process for setting goals and regularly checking progress toward achieving those goals. It is a continual feedback process whereby the actual outputs are measured and compared with the desired goals. Any discrepancy or gap is then fed back into changing the inputs of the process, so as to achieve the desired goals or outputs.
   a. Performance management
   b. 28-hour day
   c. 1990 Clean Air Act
   d. 33 Strategies of War

46. In psychology research on behaviorism, _____ are scales used to report performance. _____ are normally presented vertically with scale points ranging from five to nine.

Chapter 9. Human Resource Management: Getting the Right People for Managerial Success

It is an appraisal method that aims to combine the benefits of narratives, critical incident incidents, and quantified ratings by anchoring a quantified scale with specific narrative examples of good or poor performance.

a. 1990 Clean Air Act
b. Behaviorally anchored rating scales
c. 28-hour day
d. 33 Strategies of War

47. _____ is a process of agreeing upon objectives within an organization so that management and employees agree to the objectives and understand what they are in the organization.

The term '_____' was first popularized by Peter Drucker in his 1954 book 'The Practice of Management'.

The essence of _____ is participative goal setting, choosing course of actions and decision making.

a. Clean sheet review
b. Job enrichment
c. Business economics
d. Management by objectives

48. A _____ is a set of categories designed to elicit information about a quantitative or a qualitative attribute. In the social sciences, common examples are the Likert scale and 1-10 _____s in which a person selects the number which is considered to reflect the perceived quality of a product.

A _____ is an instrument that requires the rater to assign the rated object that have numerals assigned to them.

a. Rating scale
b. Thurstone scale
c. Polytomous Rasch model
d. Spearman-Brown prediction formula

49. In finance, an _____ is a contract between a buyer and a seller that gives the buyer the right--but not the obligation-- to buy or to sell a particular asset (the underlying asset) at a later day at an agreed price. In return for granting the _____, the seller collects a payment (the premium) from the buyer. A call _____ gives the buyer the right to buy the underlying asset; a put _____ gives the buyer of the _____ the right to sell the underlying asset.

a. A4e
b. AAAI
c. A Stake in the Outcome
d. Option

50. A _____ is an agreement between a company and an employee (usually upper executive) specifying that the employee will receive certain significant benefits if employment is terminated. Sometimes, certain conditions, typically a change in company ownership, must be met, but often the cause of termination is unspecified. These benefits may include severance pay, cash bonuses, stock options, or other benefits.

a. Job hunting
b. Career development
c. First-mover advantage
d. Golden parachute

51. An _____ is a formal scheme used to promote or encourage specific actions or behavior by a specific group of people during a defined period of time. _____s are particularly used in business management to motivate employees, and in sales in order to attract and retain customers. The scientific literature also refers to this concept as Pay for Performance.

Chapter 9. Human Resource Management: Getting the Right People for Managerial Success

a. A4e
b. Incentive program
c. AAAI
d. A Stake in the Outcome

52. The 'business case for _____', theorizes that in a global marketplace, a company that employs a diverse workforce (both men and women, people of many generations, people from ethnically and racially diverse backgrounds etc.) is better able to understand the demographics of the marketplace it serves and is thus better equipped to thrive in that marketplace than a company that has a more limited range of employee demographics.

An additional corollary suggests that a company that supports the _____ of its workforce can also improve employee satisfaction, productivity and retention.

a. Virtual team
b. Trademark
c. Diversity
d. Kanban

53. _____ attempts to explain relational satisfaction in terms of perceptions of fair/unfair distributions of resources within interpersonal relationships. _____ is considered as one of the justice theories, It was first developed in 1962 by John Stacey Adams, a workplace and behavioral psychologist, who asserted that employees seek to maintain equity between the inputs that they bring to a job and the outcomes that they receive from it against the perceived inputs and outcomes of others (Adams, 1965.) The belief is that people value fair treatment which causes them to be motivated to keep the fairness maintained within the relationships of their co-workers and the organization.

a. A4e
b. AAAI
c. A Stake in the Outcome
d. Equity theory

54. _____ is the act by an employer of terminating employment. Though such a decision can be made by an employer for a variety of reasons, ranging from an economic downturn to performance-related problems on the part of the employee, being fired has a strong stigma in many cultures. To be fired, as opposed to quitting voluntarily (or being laid off), is often perceived as being the employee's fault, and is therefore considered to be disgraceful and a sign of failure.

a. Firing
b. Termination of employment
c. Layoff
d. Severance package

55. _____ is the temporary suspension or permanent termination of employment of an employee or (more commonly) a group of employees for business reasons, such as the decision that certain positions are no longer necessary or a business slow-down or interruption in work. Originally the term '_____' referred exclusively to a temporary interruption in work, as when factory work cyclically falls off. However, in recent times the term can also refer to the permanent elimination of a position.

a. Retirement
b. Wrongful dismissal
c. Layoff
d. Termination of employment

56. _____ is a term defined by the Oxford English Dictionary as an individual's 'course or progress through life '. It is usually considered to pertain to remunerative work (and sometimes also formal education.)

The etymology of the term is somewhat ironic in that it comes from the Latin word carrera, which means race .

a. Spatial mismatch
b. Career
c. Nursing shortage
d. Career planning

57. As defined by Richard Beckhard, _____ is a planned, top-down, organization-wide effort to increase the organization's effectiveness and health. _____ is achieved through interventions in the organization's 'processes,' using behavioural science knowledge. According to Warren Bennis, _____ is a complex strategy intended to change the beliefs, attitudes, values, and structure of organizations so that they can better adapt to new technologies, markets, and challenges.
   a. Informal organization
   b. Organizational culture
   c. Organizational structure
   d. Organizational development

Chapter 10. Organizational Change & Innovation

1. The _____ is a general business term describing the largest group of consumers for a specified industry product. It is the opposite extreme of the term niche market.

The _____ is the group of consumers who occupy the overwhelming mass of a bell curve for common household products, i.e. they could be tagged as being 'average'.

   a. Chief legal officer
   b. Chief analytics officer
   c. Supervisory board
   d. Mass market

2. The term '_____' refers to the concept of collecting information and attempting to spot a pattern in the information. In some fields of study, the term '_____' has more formally-defined meanings.

In project management _____ is a mathematical technique that uses historical results to predict future outcome.

   a. Regression analysis
   b. Least squares
   c. Stepwise regression
   d. Trend analysis

3. _____ in its literal sense is the process of transformation of local or regional phenomena into global ones. It can be described as a process by which the people of the world are unified into a single society and function together.

This process is a combination of economic, technological, sociocultural and political forces.

   a. Histogram
   b. Cost Management
   c. Collaborative Planning, Forecasting and Replenishment
   d. Globalization

4. _____ is the strategic and coherent approach to the management of an organisation's most valued assets - the people working there who individually and collectively contribute to the achievement of the objectives of the business. The terms '_____' and 'human resources' (HR) have largely replaced the term 'personnel management' as a description of the processes involved in managing people in organizations. In simple sense, _____ means employing people, developing their resources, utilizing, maintaining and compensating their services in tune with the job and organizational requirement.

   a. Progressive discipline
   b. Human resource management
   c. Job knowledge
   d. Revolving door syndrome

5. _____ describes the relocation by a company of a business process from one country to another -- typically an operational process, such as manufacturing such as accounting. Even state governments employ _____.

The term is in use in several distinct but closely related ways.

   a. A4e
   b. A Stake in the Outcome
   c. AAAI
   d. Offshoring

6. _____ is subcontracting a process, such as product design or manufacturing, to a third-party company. The decision to outsource is often made in the interest of lowering cost or making better use of time and energy costs, redirecting or conserving energy directed at the competencies of a particular business, or to make more efficient use of land, labor, capital, (information) technology and resources. _____ became part of the business lexicon during the 1980s.

  a. Unemployment insurance
  b. Operant conditioning
  c. Opinion leadership
  d. Outsourcing

7. _____ is a term defined by the Oxford English Dictionary as an individual's 'course or progress through life '. It is usually considered to pertain to remunerative work (and sometimes also formal education.)

The etymology of the term is somewhat ironic in that it comes from the Latin word carrera, which means race .

  a. Spatial mismatch
  b. Nursing shortage
  c. Career planning
  d. Career

8. _____ is, in very basic words, a position a firm occupies against its competitors.

According to Michael Porter, the three methods for creating a sustainable _____ are through:

1. Cost leadership

2. Differentiation

3. Focus (economics)

  a. Theory Z
  b. 1990 Clean Air Act
  c. 28-hour day
  d. Competitive advantage

9. _____ or _____ data refers to selected population characteristics as used in government, marketing or opinion research, or the _____ profiles used in such research. Note the distinction from the term 'demography' Commonly-used _____s include race, age, income, disabilities, mobility (in terms of travel time to work or number of vehicles available), educational attainment, home ownership, employment status, and even location.

  a. Affiliation
  b. Abraham Harold Maslow
  c. Adam Smith
  d. Demographic

10. _____ describes how content an individual is with his or her job.

The happier people are within their job, the more satisfied they are said to be. _____ is not the same as motivation, although it is clearly linked.

  a. Human relations
  b. Goal-setting theory
  c. Job analysis
  d. Job satisfaction

11. In economics and sociology, an _____ is any factor (financial or non-financial) that enables or motivates a particular course of action, or counts as a reason for preferring one choice to the alternatives. It is an expectation that encourages people to behave in a certain way. Since human beings are purposeful creatures, the study of _____ structures is central to the study of all economic activity (both in terms of individual decision-making and in terms of co-operation and competition within a larger institutional structure.)

   a. A4e
   b. A Stake in the Outcome
   c. AAAI
   d. Incentive

12. _____ is a method by which the job performance of an employee is evaluated _____ is a part of career development.

_____s are regular reviews of employee performance within organizations

Generally, the aims of a _____ are to:

- Give feedback on performance to employees.
- Identify employee training needs.
- Document criteria used to allocate organizational rewards.
- Form a basis for personnel decisions: salary increases, promotions, disciplinary actions, etc.
- Provide the opportunity for organizational diagnosis and development.
- Facilitate communication between employee and administraton
- Validate selection techniques and human resource policies to meet federal Equal Employment Opportunity requirements.

A common approach to assessing performance is to use a numerical or scalar rating system whereby managers are asked to score an individual against a number of objectives/attributes. In some companies, employees receive assessments from their manager, peers, subordinates and customers while also performing a self assessment.

   a. Personnel management
   b. Performance appraisal
   c. Human resource management
   d. Progressive discipline

13. The phrase _____ refers to the aspect of corporate strategy, corporate finance and management dealing with the buying, selling and combining of different companies that can aid, finance, or help a growing company in a given industry grow rapidly without having to create another business entity.

An acquisition, also known as a takeover or a buyout, is the buying of one company (the 'target') by another. An acquisition may be friendly or hostile.

   a. 28-hour day
   b. 33 Strategies of War
   c. 1990 Clean Air Act
   d. Mergers and acquisitions

14. An _____ is a mostly hierarchical concept of subordination of entities that collaborate and contribute to serve one common aim.

Organizations are a variant of clustered entities. The structure of an organization is usually set up in many a styles, dependent on their objectives and ambience.

a. Open shop
c. Organizational development
b. Informal organization
d. Organizational structure

15. The phrase mergers and _____s refers to the aspect of corporate strategy, corporate finance and management dealing with the buying, selling and combining of different companies that can aid, finance, or help a growing company in a given industry grow rapidly without having to create another business entity.

An _____, also known as a takeover or a buyout, is the buying of one company (the 'target') by another. An _____ may be friendly or hostile.

a. AAAI
c. A Stake in the Outcome
b. A4e
d. Acquisition

16. _____. The objective of OD is to improve the organization's capacity to handle its internal and external functioning and relationships. This would include such things as improved interpersonal and group processes, more effective communication, enhanced ability to cope with organizational problems of all kinds, more effective decision processes, more appropriate leadership style, improved skill in dealing with destructive conflict, and higher levels of trust and cooperation among organizational members.

a. Organizational development
c. Organizational structure
b. Industrial relations
d. Improved Organizational Performance

17. As defined by Richard Beckhard, _____ is a planned, top-down, organization-wide effort to increase the organization's effectiveness and health. _____ is achieved through interventions in the organization's 'processes,' using behavioural science knowledge. According to Warren Bennis, _____ is a complex strategy intended to change the beliefs, attitudes, values, and structure of organizations so that they can better adapt to new technologies, markets, and challenges.

a. Informal organization
c. Organizational culture
b. Organizational structure
d. Organizational development

18. In statistics, _____ is:

- the arithmetic _____
- the expected value of a random variable, which is also called the population _____.

It is sometimes stated that the '_____' _____s average. This is incorrect if '_____' is taken in the specific sense of 'arithmetic _____' as there are different types of averages: the _____, median, and mode. Other simple statistical analyses use measures of spread, such as range, interquartile range, or standard deviation. For a real-valued random variable X, the _____ is the expectation of X. Note that not every probability distribution has a defined _____; see the Cauchy distribution for an example.

a. Control chart
c. Correlation
b. Statistical inference
d. Mean

19. In economics, a _____ exists when a specific individual or enterprise has sufficient control over a particular product or service to determine significantly the terms on which other individuals shall have access to it. Monopolies are thus characterized by a lack of economic competition for the good or service that they provide and a lack of viable substitute goods. The verb 'monopolize' refers to the process by which a firm gains persistently greater market share than what is expected under perfect competition.
   a. 28-hour day
   c. 33 Strategies of War
   b. 1990 Clean Air Act
   d. Monopoly

20. The process of _____ involves the introduction of a good or service that is new or substantially improved. This includes, but is not limited to, improvements in functional characteristics, technical abilities, or ease of use.
   a. Service-profit chain
   c. Job enlargement
   b. Product innovation
   d. Letter of resignation

21. In decision theory and estimation theory, the _____ of an estimator, $\hat{\theta}$, of an unknown parameter of the distribution, θ, is the expected value of the loss function

$$R(\theta, \hat{\theta}) = \mathbb{E}_\theta L(\theta, \hat{\theta}) = \int L(\theta, \hat{\theta})\, dP_\theta.$$

where dP_θ is a probability measure parametrized by θ.

- For a scalar parameter θ and a quadratic loss function,

$$L(\theta, \hat{\theta}) = (\theta - \hat{\theta})^2$$

the _____ function becomes the mean squared error of the estimate,

$$R(\theta, \hat{\theta}) = E_\theta(\theta - \hat{\theta})^2$$

- In density estimation, the unknown parameter is probability density itself. The loss function is typically chosen to be a norm in an appropriate function space. For example, for L^2 norm,

$$L(f, \hat{f}) = \|f - \hat{f}\|_2^2$$

the _____ function becomes the mean integrated squared error

$$R(f, \hat{f}) = E\|f - \hat{f}\|^2$$

Chapter 10. Organizational Change & Innovation

a. Financial modeling
b. Risk aversion
c. Linear model
d. Risk

22. _____ is one of the managerial functions like planning, organizing, staffing and directing. It is an important function because it helps to check the errors and to take the corrective action so that deviation from standards are minimized and stated goals of the organization are achieved in desired manner.According to modern concepts, _____ is a foreseeing action whereas earlier concept of _____ was used only when errors were detected. _____ in management means setting standards, measuring actual performance and taking corrective action.

a. Turnover
b. Decision tree pruning
c. Control
d. Schedule of reinforcement

23. _____ is an idea in the field of Organizational studies and management which describes the psychology, attitudes, experiences, beliefs and Values (personal and cultural values) of an organization. It has been defined as 'the specific collection of values and norms that are shared by people and groups in an organization and that control the way they interact with each other and with stakeholders outside the organization.'

This definition continues to explain organizational values also known as 'beliefs and ideas about what kinds of goals members of an organization should pursue and ideas about the appropriate kinds or standards of behavior organizational members should use to achieve these goals. From organizational values develop organizational norms, guidelines or expectations that prescribe appropriate kinds of behavior by employees in particular situations and control the behavior of organizational members towards one another.'

_____ is not the same as corporate culture.

a. Organizational development
b. Organizational effectiveness
c. Union shop
d. Organizational culture

24. _____ according to Onuoha (2007) is the practice of starting new organizations or revitalizing mature organizations, particularly new businesses generally in response to identified opportunities. _____ is often a difficult undertaking, as a vast majority of new businesses fail. Entrepreneurial activities are substantially different depending on the type of organization that is being started.

a. A4e
b. Entrepreneurship
c. AAAI
d. A Stake in the Outcome

25. Engineering _____ is the permissible limit of variation in

1. a physical dimension,
2. a measured value or physical property of a material, manufactured object, system, or service,
3. other measured values (such as temperature, humidity, etc.)
4. in engineering and safety, a physical distance or space (_____), as in a truck (lorry), train or boat under a bridge as well as a train in a tunnel

Dimensions, properties, or conditions may vary within certain practical limits without significantly affecting functioning of equipment or a process. _____s are specified to allow reasonable leeway for imperfections and inherent variability without compromising performance.

The _____ may be specified as a factor or percentage of the nominal value, a maximum deviation from a nominal value, an explicit range of allowed values, be specified by a note or published standard with this information, or be implied by the numeric accuracy of the nominal value. _____ can be symmetrical, as in 40±0.1, or asymmetrical, such as 40+0.2/−0.1.

- a. Root cause analysis
- b. Quality assurance
- c. Zero defects
- d. Tolerance

26. _____ is a business management strategy, initially implemented by Motorola, that today enjoys widespread application in many sectors of industry.

_____ seeks to improve the quality of process outputs by identifying and removing the causes of defects (errors) and variation in manufacturing and business processes. It uses a set of quality management methods, including statistical methods, and creates a special infrastructure of people within the organization ('Black Belts' etc.)

- a. Production line
- b. Takt time
- c. Six Sigma
- d. Theory of constraints

27. _____ plant, and equipment, is a term used in accountancy for assets and property which cannot easily be converted into cash. This can be compared with current assets such as cash or bank accounts, which are described as liquid assets. In most cases, only tangible assets are referred to as fixed.

- a. 28-hour day
- b. 33 Strategies of War
- c. 1990 Clean Air Act
- d. Fixed asset

28. _____ is a structured approach to transitioning individuals, teams, and organizations from a current state to a desired future state. The current definition of _____ includes both organizational _____ processes and individual _____ models, which together are used to manage the people side of change.

A number of models are available for understanding the transitioning of individuals through the phases of _____ and strengthening organizational development initiative in both government and corporate sectors.

- a. 28-hour day
- b. Change management
- c. 33 Strategies of War
- d. 1990 Clean Air Act

29. _____ is the probability that an individual will keep his or her job; a job with a high level of _____ is such that a person with the job would have a small chance of becoming unemployed.

_____ is dependent on economy, prevailing business conditions, and the individual's personal skills. It has been found that people have more _____ in times of economic expansion and less in times of a recession.

- a. Hygiene factors
- b. Just cause
- c. Job security
- d. Multiple careers

Chapter 10. Organizational Change & Innovation

30. _____ is the process of comparing the cost, cycle time, productivity, or quality of a specific process or method to another that is widely considered to be an industry standard or best practice. Essentially, _____ provides a snapshot of the performance of your business and helps you understand where you are in relation to a particular standard. The result is often a business case for making changes in order to make improvements.
   a. Cost leadership
   b. Complementors
   c. Benchmarking
   d. Competitive heterogeneity

31. _____ refers to metrics and measures of output from production processes, per unit of input. Labor _____, for example, is typically measured as a ratio of output per labor-hour, an input. _____ may be conceived of as a metrics of the technical or engineering efficiency of production.
   a. Remanufacturing
   b. Value engineering
   c. Master production schedule
   d. Productivity

32. _____ has been described as the 'process of social influence in which one person can enlist the aid and support of others in the accomplishment of a common task'. A definition more inclusive of followers comes from Alan Keith of Genentech who said '_____ is ultimately about creating a way for people to contribute to making something extraordinary happen.'

_____ is one of the most salient aspects of the organizational context. However, defining _____ has been challenging.

   a. 28-hour day
   b. 1990 Clean Air Act
   c. Situational leadership
   d. Leadership

Chapter 11. Managing Individual Differences & Behavior: Supervising People as People

1. _____ is a term defined by the Oxford English Dictionary as an individual's 'course or progress through life '. It is usually considered to pertain to remunerative work (and sometimes also formal education.)

The etymology of the term is somewhat ironic in that it comes from the Latin word carrera, which means race .

   a. Spatial mismatch   b. Career
   c. Nursing shortage   d. Career planning

2. _____ describes the situation when output from (or information about the result of) an event or phenomenon in the past will influence the same event/phenomenon in the present or future. When an event is part of a chain of cause-and-effect that forms a circuit or loop, then the event is said to 'feed back' into itself.

_____ is also a synonym for:

- _____ signal; the information about the initial event that is the basis for subsequent modification of the event.
- _____ loop; the causal path that leads from the initial generation of the _____ signal to the subsequent modification of the event.

_____ is a mechanism, process or signal that is looped back to control a system within itself. Such a loop is called a _____ loop.

   a. 1990 Clean Air Act   b. Positive feedback
   c. Feedback loop   d. Feedback

3. _____, commonly abbreviated to Gen X, is a term used to refer to a generational cohort of children born after the baby boom ended and usually prior to the 1980s

The term _____ has been used in demography, the social sciences, and marketing, though it is most often used in popular culture.

In the U.S. _____ was originally referred to as the 'baby bust' generation because of the drop in the birth rate following the baby boom.

   a. Affiliation   b. Adam Smith
   c. Abraham Harold Maslow   d. Generation X

4. _____ is a term used to describe the demographic cohort following Generation X. Its members are often referred to as 'Millennials' or 'Echo Boomers') . There are no precise dates for when Gen Y begins and ends. Most commentators use dates from the early 1980s to early 1990s.
   a. Benjamin R. Barber   b. David Wittig
   c. Giovanni Agnelli   d. Generation Y

Chapter 11. Managing Individual Differences & Behavior: Supervising People as People

5. _____ is the strategic and coherent approach to the management of an organisation's most valued assets - the people working there who individually and collectively contribute to the achievement of the objectives of the business. The terms '_____' and 'human resources' (HR) have largely replaced the term 'personnel management' as a description of the processes involved in managing people in organizations. In simple sense, _____ means employing people, developing their resources, utilizing, maintaining and compensating their services in tune with the job and organizational requirement.

   a. Job knowledge
   b. Revolving door syndrome
   c. Progressive discipline
   d. Human resource management

6. _____ describes how content an individual is with his or her job.

The happier people are within their job, the more satisfied they are said to be. _____ is not the same as motivation, although it is clearly linked.

   a. Job satisfaction
   b. Goal-setting theory
   c. Human relations
   d. Job analysis

7. _____ has been described as the 'process of social influence in which one person can enlist the aid and support of others in the accomplishment of a common task'. A definition more inclusive of followers comes from Alan Keith of Genentech who said '_____ is ultimately about creating a way for people to contribute to making something extraordinary happen.'

_____ is one of the most salient aspects of the organizational context. However, defining _____ has been challenging.

   a. Situational leadership
   b. 1990 Clean Air Act
   c. Leadership
   d. 28-hour day

8. The trait of _____ is a central dimension of human personality. Extraverts (also spelled extroverts) tend to be gregarious, assertive, and interested in seeking out excitement. Introverts, in contrast, tend to be more reserved, less outgoing, and less sociable.

   a. A4e
   b. A Stake in the Outcome
   c. AAAI
   d. Extraversion-introversion

9. _____ is one of five major domains of personality discovered by psychologists. Openness involves active imagination, aesthetic sensitivity, attentiveness to inner feelings, preference for variety, and intellectual curiosity. A great deal of psychometric research has demonstrated that these qualities are statistically correlated.

   a. Extraversion
   b. Introverts
   c. Introversion
   d. Openness to experience

10. _____ is one of the managerial functions like planning, organizing, staffing and directing. It is an important function because it helps to check the errors and to take the corrective action so that deviation from standards are minimized and stated goals of the organization are achieved in desired manner. According to modern concepts, _____ is a foreseeing action whereas earlier concept of _____ was used only when errors were detected. _____ in management means setting standards, measuring actual performance and taking corrective action.

a. Turnover
b. Decision tree pruning
c. Schedule of reinforcement
d. Control

11. _____ is a term in psychology which refers to a person's belief about what causes the good or bad results in his or her life, either in general or in a specific area such as health or academics. Understanding of the concept was developed by Julian B. Rotter in 1954, and has since become an important aspect of personality studies.

_____ refers to the extent to which individuals believe that they can control events that affect them.

a. Self-enhancement
b. Locus of control
c. Machiavellianism
d. Social loafing

12. In economics and sociology, an _____ is any factor (financial or non-financial) that enables or motivates a particular course of action, or counts as a reason for preferring one choice to the alternatives. It is an expectation that encourages people to behave in a certain way. Since human beings are purposeful creatures, the study of _____ structures is central to the study of all economic activity (both in terms of individual decision-making and in terms of co-operation and competition within a larger institutional structure.)

a. AAAI
b. A4e
c. A Stake in the Outcome
d. Incentive

13. _____ is the belief that one is capable of performing in a certain manner to attain certain goals. It is a belief that one has the capabilities to execute the courses of actions required to manage prospective situations. Unlike efficacy, which is the power to produce an effect (in essence, competence), _____ is the belief (whether or not accurate) that one has the power to produce that effect.

a. 1990 Clean Air Act
b. 28-hour day
c. 33 Strategies of War
d. Self-efficacy

14. In psychology, _____ reflects a person's overall evaluation or appraisal of his or her own worth.

_____ encompasses beliefs (for example, 'I am competent/incompetent') and emotions (for example, triumph/despair, pride/shame.) Behavior may reflect _____

a. 28-hour day
b. 1990 Clean Air Act
c. 33 Strategies of War
d. Self-esteem

15. _____, often measured as an _____ Quotient (EQ), is a term that describes the ability, capacity, skill or (in the case of the trait _____ model) a self-perceived ability, to identify, assess, and manage the emotions of one's self, of others, and of groups. Different models have been proposed for the definition of _____ and disagreement exists as to how the term should be used. Despite these disagreements, which are often highly technical, the ability _____ and trait _____ models (but not the mixed models) are enjoying considerable support in the literature and have successful applications in many different domains.

a. Emotional intelligence
b. A4e
c. AAAI
d. A Stake in the Outcome

Chapter 11. Managing Individual Differences & Behavior: Supervising People as People

16. Social consciousness is consciousness shared within a society. It can also be defined as _____; to be aware of the problems that different societies and communities face on a day-to-day basis; to be conscious of the difficulties and hardships of society.

There is debate as to exactly what the term means.

a. Self-disclosure
b. Role conflict
c. Soft skill
d. Social awareness

17. _____ is an uncomfortable feeling caused by holding two contradictory ideas simultaneously. The 'ideas' or 'cognitions' in question may include attitudes and beliefs, and also the awareness of one's behavior. The theory of _____ proposes that people have a motivational drive to reduce dissonance by changing their attitudes, beliefs, and behaviors, or by justifying or rationalizing their attitudes, beliefs, and behaviors.

a. Trait theory
b. Cognitive bias
c. Quantitative psychology
d. Cognitive dissonance

18. _____ refers to metrics and measures of output from production processes, per unit of input. Labor _____, for example, is typically measured as a ratio of output per labor-hour, an input. _____ may be conceived of as a metrics of the technical or engineering efficiency of production.

a. Remanufacturing
b. Master production schedule
c. Value engineering
d. Productivity

19. _____ is a habitual pattern of absence from a duty or obligation.

Frequent absence from the workplace may be indicative of poor morale or of sick building syndrome. However, many employers have implemented absence policies which make no distinction between absences for genuine illness and absence for inappropriate reasons.

a. Absenteeism
b. Emanation of the state
c. A4e
d. A Stake in the Outcome

20. The _____ is a form of reactivity whereby subjects improve an aspect of their behavior being experimentally measured simply in response to the fact that they are being studied, not in response to any particular experimental manipulation.

The term was coined in 1955 by Henry A. Landsberger when analyzing older experiments from 1924-1932 at the Hawthorne Works (outside Chicago.) Hawthorne Works had commissioned a study to see if its workers would become more productive in higher or lower levels of light.

a. 1990 Clean Air Act
b. Hawthorne effect
c. 33 Strategies of War
d. 28-hour day

Chapter 11. Managing Individual Differences & Behavior: Supervising People as People

21. _____ are a special type of work behavior that are defined as individual behaviors that are beneficial to the organization and are discretionary, not directly or explicitly recognized by the formal reward system. These behaviors are rather a matter of personal choice, such that their omission are not generally understood as punishable. _____ are thought to have an important impact on the effectiveness and efficiency of work teams and organizations, therefore contributing to the overall productivity of the organization.

   a. A4e
   b. AAAI
   c. Organizational citizenship behaviors
   d. A Stake in the Outcome

22. In a human resources context, _____ or labor _____ is the rate at which an employer gains and loses employees. Simple ways to describe it are 'how long employees tend to stay' or 'the rate of traffic through the revolving door.' _____ is measured for individual companies and for their industry as a whole. If an employer is said to have a high _____ relative to its competitors, it means that employees of that company have a shorter average tenure than those of other companies in the same industry.

   a. Continuous
   b. Career portfolios
   c. Ten year occupational employment projection
   d. Turnover

23. In economics, business, retail, and accounting, a _____ is the value of money that has been used up to produce something, and hence is not available for use anymore. In economics, a _____ is an alternative that is given up as a result of a decision. In business, the _____ may be one of acquisition, in which case the amount of money expended to acquire it is counted as _____.

   a. Cost allocation
   b. Cost overrun
   c. Cost
   d. Fixed costs

24. The 'business case for _____', theorizes that in a global marketplace, a company that employs a diverse workforce (both men and women, people of many generations, people from ethnically and racially diverse backgrounds etc.) is better able to understand the demographics of the marketplace it serves and is thus better equipped to thrive in that marketplace than a company that has a more limited range of employee demographics.

   An additional corollary suggests that a company that supports the _____ of its workforce can also improve employee satisfaction, productivity and retention.

   a. Virtual team
   b. Kanban
   c. Trademark
   d. Diversity

25. The _____ refers to a cognitive bias whereby the perception of a particular trait is influenced by the perception of the former traits in a sequence of interpretations.

   Edward L. Thorndike was the first to support the _____ with empirical research. In a psychology study published in 1920, Thorndike asked commanding officers to rate their soldiers; Thorndike found high cross-correlation between all positive and all negative traits.

   a. Distinction bias
   b. Sunk costs
   c. Halo effect
   d. Cognitive biases

Chapter 11. Managing Individual Differences & Behavior: Supervising People as People

26. A _____ occurs when people attribute their successes to internal or personal factors but attribute their failures to situational factors beyond their control. The _____ can be seen in the common human tendency to take credit for success but to deny responsibility for failure. It may also manifest itself as a tendency for people to evaluate ambiguous information in a way that is beneficial to their interests.

    a. Pygmalion effect
    b. Fundamental attribution error
    c. Halo effect
    d. Self-serving bias

27. The _____ refers to situations in which students perform better than other students simply because they are expected to do so. The effect is named after George Bernard Shaw's play Pygmalion, in which a professor makes a bet that he can teach a poor flower girl to speak and act like an upper-class lady, and is successful.

The _____ requires a student to internalize the expectations of their superiors.

    a. Confirmation bias
    b. Pygmalion effect
    c. Halo effect
    d. Distinction bias

28. _____ is the temporary suspension or permanent termination of employment of an employee or (more commonly) a group of employees for business reasons, such as the decision that certain positions are no longer necessary or a business slow-down or interruption in work. Originally the term '_____' referred exclusively to a temporary interruption in work, as when factory work cyclically falls off. However, in recent times the term can also refer to the permanent elimination of a position.

    a. Retirement
    b. Wrongful dismissal
    c. Termination of employment
    d. Layoff

29. _____ is the probability that an individual will keep his or her job; a job with a high level of _____ is such that a person with the job would have a small chance of becoming unemployed.

_____ is dependent on economy, prevailing business conditions, and the individual's personal skills. It has been found that people have more _____ in times of economic expansion and less in times of a recession.

    a. Job security
    b. Hygiene factors
    c. Just cause
    d. Multiple careers

30. '_____ is a conflict among the roles corresponding to two or more statuses.'

_____ is a special form of social conflict that takes place when one is forced to take on two different and incompatible roles at the same time. Consider the example of a doctor who is himself a patient, or who must decide whether he should be present for his daughter's birthday party (in his role as 'father') or attend an ailing patient (as 'doctor'.) (Also compare the psychological concept of cognitive dissonance.)

    a. Self-disclosure
    b. Soft skill
    c. Social network analysis
    d. Role conflict

31. In economics, _____ is the desire to own something and the ability to pay for it. The term _____ signifies the ability or the willingness to buy a particular commodity at a given point of time.

Chapter 11. Managing Individual Differences & Behavior: Supervising People as People

  a. 33 Strategies of War   b. 1990 Clean Air Act
  c. Demand   d. 28-hour day

32. _____ and career coaching are similar in nature to traditional counseling (Kim, Li, Lian, 2002.) However, the focus is generally on issues such as career exploration, career change, personal career development and other career related issues (Swanson, 1995.) Typically when people come for _____ they know exactly what they want to get out of the process, but are unsure about how it will work (Galassi, Crace, Martin, James, and Wallace, 1992.)

  a. Career counseling   b. 1990 Clean Air Act
  c. 33 Strategies of War   d. 28-hour day

33. _____ are employee benefit programs offered by many employers, typically in conjunction with a health insurance plan. _____s are intended to help employees deal with personal problems that might adversely impact their work performance, health, and well-being. _____s generally include assessment, short-term counseling and referral services for employees and their household members.

  a. A Stake in the Outcome   b. Employee benefits
  c. Employee assistance programs   d. A4e

34. The _____ is one of the most frequently used personality tests in mental health. The test is used by trained professionals to assist in identifying personality structure and psychopathology.

The original authors of the _____ were Starke R. Hathaway, PhD, and J. C. McKinley, MD.

  a. Minnesota Multiphasic Personality Inventory   b. 1990 Clean Air Act
  c. 28-hour day   d. Thematic Apperception Test

Chapter 12. Motivating Employees: Achieving Superior Performance in the Workplace 107

1. An _____ is any party that makes an investment.

The term has taken on a specific meaning in finance to describe the particular types of people and companies that regularly purchase equity or debt securities for financial gain in exchange for funding an expanding company. Less frequently, the term is applied to parties who purchase real estate, currency, commodity derivatives, personal property, or other assets.

   a. AAAI
   b. Investor
   c. A Stake in the Outcome
   d. A4e

2. _____ describes the situation when output from (or information about the result of) an event or phenomenon in the past will influence the same event/phenomenon in the present or future. When an event is part of a chain of cause-and-effect that forms a circuit or loop, then the event is said to 'feed back' into itself.

   _____ is also a synonym for:

   - _____ signal; the information about the initial event that is the basis for subsequent modification of the event.
   - _____ loop; the causal path that leads from the initial generation of the _____ signal to the subsequent modification of the event.

   _____ is a mechanism, process or signal that is looped back to control a system within itself. Such a loop is called a _____ loop.

   a. 1990 Clean Air Act
   b. Positive feedback
   c. Feedback loop
   d. Feedback

3. In economics and sociology, an _____ is any factor (financial or non-financial) that enables or motivates a particular course of action, or counts as a reason for preferring one choice to the alternatives. It is an expectation that encourages people to behave in a certain way. Since human beings are purposeful creatures, the study of _____ structures is central to the study of all economic activity (both in terms of individual decision-making and in terms of co-operation and competition within a larger institutional structure.)

   a. A Stake in the Outcome
   b. Incentive
   c. AAAI
   d. A4e

4. Maslow's _____ is a theory in psychology, proposed by Abraham Maslow in his 1943 paper A Theory of Human Motivation, which he subsequently extended to include his observations of humans' innate curiosity.

Maslow's _____ is predetermined in order of importance. It is often depicted as a pyramid consisting of five levels: the lowest level is associated with physiological needs, while the uppermost level is associated with self-actualization needs, particularly those related to identity and purpose. Deficiency needs must be met first. Once these are met, seeking to satisfy growth needs drives personal growth. The higher needs in this hierarchy only come into focus when the lower needs in the pyramid are met.

Chapter 12. Motivating Employees: Achieving Superior Performance in the Workplace

a. 33 Strategies of War
c. Hierarchy of needs

b. 28-hour day
d. 1990 Clean Air Act

5. _____ is a term that has been used in various psychology theories, often in slightly different ways (e.g., Goldstein, Maslow, Rogers.) The term was originally introduced by the organismic theorist Kurt Goldstein for the motive to realise all of one's potentialities. In his view, it is the master motive--indeed, the only real motive a person has, all others being merely manifestations of it.

a. 33 Strategies of War
c. 28-hour day

b. 1990 Clean Air Act
d. Self-actualization

6. Clayton Paul Alderfer is an American psychologist who further expanded Maslow's hierarchy of needs by categorizing the hierarchy into his _____ Alderfer categorized the lower order needs (Physiological and Safety) into the Existence category. He fit Maslow's interpersonal love and esteem needs into the relatedness category. The growth category contained the Self Actualization and self esteem needs.

Alderfer also proposed a regression theory to go along with the _____. He said that when needs in a higher category are not met then individuals redouble the efforts invested in a lower category need.

a. ERG theory
c. Alvin Neill Jackson

b. Adam Smith
d. Abraham Harold Maslow

7. _____ is a term coined by Deborah E. Meyerson used to describe corporate professionals who work toward positive change in both their work environment and the way their companies conduct business -- often taking 'radical' action that is just short of getting them fired.

In her book, _____: How Everyday Leaders Inspire Change at Work (Harvard Business School Press), Meyerson describes employees who believe and work toward creating adaptive, family-friendly, and socially responsible workplaces.

_____ are quiet leaders that act as catalysts for new ideas, alternative perspectives, and organizational learning and change -- and balance company conformity with individual rebellion.

a. 1990 Clean Air Act
c. 28-hour day

b. 33 Strategies of War
d. Tempered radicals

8. In law, _____ is the term to describe a partnership between two or more parties.

In England a number of statutes on the subject have been passed, the chief being the Bastardy Act of 1845, and the Bastardy Laws Amendment Acts of 1872 and 1873. The mother of a bastard may summon the putative father to petty sessions within twelve months of the birth (or at any later time if he is proved to have contributed to the child's support within twelve months after the birth), and the justices, as after hearing evidence on both sides, may, if the mother's evidence be corroborated in some material particular, adjudge the man to be the putative father of the child, and order him to pay a sum not exceeding five shillings a week for its maintenance, together with a sum for expenses incidental to the birth, or the funeral expenses, if it has died before the date of order, and the costs of the proceedings.

a. Adam Smith
b. Affirmative action
c. Abraham Harold Maslow
d. Affiliation

9. _____ is one of the managerial functions like planning, organizing, staffing and directing. It is an important function because it helps to check the errors and to take the corrective action so that deviation from standards are minimized and stated goals of the organization are achieved in desired manner. According to modern concepts, _____ is a foreseeing action whereas earlier concept of _____ was used only when errors were detected. _____ in management means setting standards, measuring actual performance and taking corrective action.

a. Schedule of reinforcement
b. Decision tree pruning
c. Turnover
d. Control

10. _____ is a term that was popularized by renowned psychologist David McClelland in 1961. However, it should be recognized that McClellend's thinking was strongly influenced by the pioneering work of Henry Murray who first identified underlying psychological human needs and motivational processes (1938.) It was Murray who set out a taxonomy of needs, including Achievement, Power and Affiliation - and placed these in the context of an integrated motivational model.

a. Need for Power
b. Two-factor theory
c. 1990 Clean Air Act
d. Need for Achievement

11. _____ refers to an individual's desire for significant accomplishment, mastering of skills, control, or high standards. The term was introduced by the psychologist, David McClelland.

_____ is related to the difficulty of tasks people choose to undertake.

a. Two-factor theory
b. 1990 Clean Air Act
c. Need for power
d. Need for achievement

12. _____ are job factors that can cause dissatisfaction if missing but do not necessarily motivate employees if increased.

_____ have mostly to do with the job environment. These factors are important or notable only when they are lacking.

a. Work system
b. Split shift
c. Work-at-home scheme
d. Hygiene factors

13. _____ describes how content an individual is with his or her job.

The happier people are within their job, the more satisfied they are said to be. _____ is not the same as motivation, although it is clearly linked.

a. Job satisfaction
b. Human relations
c. Goal-setting theory
d. Job analysis

14. _____ was developed by Frederick Herzberg, a psychologist who found that job satisfaction and job dissatisfaction acted independently of each other. _____ states that there are certain factors in the workplace that cause job satisfaction, while a separate set of factors cause dissatisfaction.

Chapter 12. Motivating Employees: Achieving Superior Performance in the Workplace

a. Need for Achievement
b. Need for power
c. 1990 Clean Air Act
d. Two-factor theory

15. _____ attempts to explain relational satisfaction in terms of perceptions of fair/unfair distributions of resources within interpersonal relationships. _____ is considered as one of the justice theories, It was first developed in 1962 by John Stacey Adams, a workplace and behavioral psychologist, who asserted that employees seek to maintain equity between the inputs that they bring to a job and the outcomes that they receive from it against the perceived inputs and outcomes of others (Adams, 1965.) The belief is that people value fair treatment which causes them to be motivated to keep the fairness maintained within the relationships of their co-workers and the organization.

a. A4e
b. Equity theory
c. AAAI
d. A Stake in the Outcome

16. _____ is the strategic and coherent approach to the management of an organisation's most valued assets - the people working there who individually and collectively contribute to the achievement of the objectives of the business. The terms '_____' and 'human resources' (HR) have largely replaced the term 'personnel management' as a description of the processes involved in managing people in organizations. In simple sense, _____ means employing people, developing their resources, utilizing, maintaining and compensating their services in tune with the job and organizational requirement.

a. Progressive discipline
b. Revolving door syndrome
c. Human resource management
d. Job knowledge

17. _____ is a method by which the job performance of an employee is evaluated _____ is a part of career development.

_____s are regular reviews of employee performance within organizations

Generally, the aims of a _____ are to:

- Give feedback on performance to employees.
- Identify employee training needs.
- Document criteria used to allocate organizational rewards.
- Form a basis for personnel decisions: salary increases, promotions, disciplinary actions, etc.
- Provide the opportunity for organizational diagnosis and development.
- Facilitate communication between employee and administraton
- Validate selection techniques and human resource policies to meet federal Equal Employment Opportunity requirements.

A common approach to assessing performance is to use a numerical or scalar rating system whereby managers are asked to score an individual against a number of objectives/attributes. In some companies, employees receive assessments from their manager, peers, subordinates and customers while also performing a self assessment.

a. Human resource management
b. Progressive discipline
c. Personnel management
d. Performance appraisal

Chapter 12. Motivating Employees: Achieving Superior Performance in the Workplace 111

18. _____ is about the mental processes regarding choice, or choosing. It explains the processes that an individual undergoes to make choices. In organizational behavior study, _____ is a motivation theory first proposed by Victor Vroom of the Yale School of Management.

a. AAAI
b. Expectancy theory
c. A4e
d. A Stake in the Outcome

19. _____ refers to metrics and measures of output from production processes, per unit of input. Labor _____, for example, is typically measured as a ratio of output per labor-hour, an input. _____ may be conceived of as a metrics of the technical or engineering efficiency of production.

a. Remanufacturing
b. Master production schedule
c. Value engineering
d. Productivity

20. _____ has become one of the most popular theories in organizational psychology.

Goal setting has been a formula used for acheivement since the early 1800s. The form and pattern has cahanged drastically over the years and there is still much debate as to what is the most efective pattern to follow.

a. Job satisfaction
b. Goal-setting theory
c. Human relations
d. Corporate Culture

21. In organizational development (OD), _____ is the application of Socio-Technical Systems principles and techniques to the humanization of work.

The aims of _____ to improved job satisfaction, to improved through-put, to improved quality and to reduced employee problems, e.g., grievances, absenteeism.

Under scientific management people would be directed by reason and the problems of industrial unrest would be appropriately (i.e., scientifically) addressed.

a. Path-goal theory
b. Management process
c. Work design
d. Graduate recruitment

22. _____ means increasing the scope of a job through extending the range of its job duties and responsibilities. This contradicts the principles of specialisation and the division of labour whereby work is divided into small units, each of which is performed repetitively by an individual worker. Some motivational theories suggest that the boredom and alienation caused by the division of labour can actually cause efficiency to fall.

a. Mock interview
b. Centralization
c. Delayering
d. Job enlargement

23. In mathematical logic, _____ is a valid argument and rule of inference which makes the inference that, if the conjunction A and B is true, then A is true, and B is true.

Chapter 12. Motivating Employees: Achieving Superior Performance in the Workplace

In formal language:

$$A \wedge B \vdash A$$

or

$$A \wedge B \vdash B$$

The argument has one premise, namely a conjunction, and one often uses _____ in longer arguments to derive one of the conjuncts.

An example in English:

    It's raining and it's pouring.

a. 1990 Clean Air Act
c. Fuzzy logic
b. Simplification
d. Validity

24. _____ is a term defined by the Oxford English Dictionary as an individual's 'course or progress through life '. It is usually considered to pertain to remunerative work (and sometimes also formal education.)

The etymology of the term is somewhat ironic in that it comes from the Latin word carrera, which means race .

a. Career
c. Career planning
b. Spatial mismatch
d. Nursing shortage

25. _____ is an attempt to motivate employees by giving them the opportunity to use the range of their abilities. It is an idea that was developed by the American psychologist Frederick Herzberg in the 1950s. It can be contrasted to job enlargement which simply increases the number of tasks without changing the challenge.

a. Job enrichment
c. C-A-K-E
b. Cash cow
d. Catfish effect

26. _____-model (SCOR(r)) is a process reference model developed by the management consulting firm PRTM and AMR Research and endorsed by the Supply-Chain Council (SCC) as the cross-industry de facto standard diagnostic tool for supply chain management. SCOR enables users to address, improve, and communicate supply chain management practices within and between all interested parties in the Extended Enterprise.

SCOR(r) is a management tool, spanning from the supplier's supplier to the customer's customer. The model has been developed by the members of the Council on a volunteer basis to describe the business activities associated with all phases of satisfying a customer's demand.

a. Supply-Chain Operations Reference
c. Delayed differentiation
b. Supply Chain Risk Management
d. Supply chain management software

Chapter 12. Motivating Employees: Achieving Superior Performance in the Workplace 113

27. _____ is the use of empirically demonstrated behavior change techniques to improve behavior, such as altering an individual's behaviors and reactions to stimuli through positive and negative reinforcement of adaptive behavior and/or the reduction of maladaptive behavior through punishment and/or therapy.

The first use of the term _____ appears to have been by Edward Thorndike in 1911

- a. Behavior modification
- b. 1990 Clean Air Act
- c. 33 Strategies of War
- d. 28-hour day

28. _____ is the use of consequences to modify the occurrence and form of behavior. _____ is distinguished from classical conditioning (also called respondent conditioning, or Pavlovian conditioning) in that _____ deals with the modification of 'voluntary behavior' or operant behavior. Operant behavior 'operates' on the environment and is maintained by its consequences, while classical conditioning deals with the conditioning of respondent behaviors which are elicited by antecedent conditions.

- a. Operant conditioning
- b. Outsourcing
- c. Unemployment insurance
- d. Occupational Safety and Health Administration

29. In operant conditioning, _____ occurs when an event following a response causes an increase in the probability of that response occurring in the future. Response strength can be assessed by measures such as the frequency with which the response is made (for example, a pigeon may peck a key more times in the session), or the speed with which it is made (for example, a rat may run a maze faster.) The environment change contingent upon the response is called a reinforcer.

- a. Diminishing Manufacturing Sources and Material Shortages
- b. Meetings, Incentives, Conferences, and Exhibitions
- c. Historiometry
- d. Reinforcement

30. _____ refers to training in different ways to improve overall performance. It takes advantage of the particular effectiveness of each training method, while at the same time attempting to neglect the shortcomings of that method by combining it with other methods that address its weaknesses.

Cross training is employee-employer field means, training employees to do one another's work.

- a. 1990 Clean Air Act
- b. 28-hour day
- c. Cross-training
- d. 33 Strategies of War

31. _____, also erroneously called Work engagement, is a widely employed, yet poorly defined concept, developed principally from the consulting community. As a result, each consulting firm asserts different definitions of the concept, component elements (commitment, job satisfaction, pride, job commitment, discretionary effort. etc), and resulting business outcomes.

- a. A4e
- b. AAAI
- c. A Stake in the Outcome
- d. Employee engagement

32. Piece work or piecework describes types of employment in which a worker is paid a fixed '_____' for each unit produced or action performed. Piece work is also a form of performance-related pay (Piece rateP) and is the oldest form of performance pay.

Chapter 12. Motivating Employees: Achieving Superior Performance in the Workplace

In a manufacturing setting, the output of piece work can be measured by the number of physical items (pieces) produced, such as when a garment worker is paid per operational step completed, regardless of the time required.

a. Piece rate
b. Scientific management
c. Methods-time measurement
d. Piecework

33. Options _____ is the practice of granting an employee stock option that is dated prior to the date that the company actually granted the option. This practice raises a number of legal and accounting issues. The practice of _____ itself is not illegal, nor is granting of discounted stock options.

a. Statistical surveys
b. Meetings, Incentives, Conferences, and Exhibitions
c. Groups decision making
d. Backdating

34. _____, when used as a special term, refers to various incentive plans introduced by businesses that provide direct or indirect payments to employees that depend on company's profitability in addition to employees' regular salary and bonuses. In publicly traded companies these plans typically amount to allocation of shares to employees.

The _____ plans are based on predetermined economic sharing rules that define the split of gains between the company as a principal and the employee as an agent.

a. Wage
b. Living wage
c. Federal Wage System
d. Profit sharing

35. In finance, an _____ is a contract between a buyer and a seller that gives the buyer the right--but not the obligation--to buy or to sell a particular asset (the underlying asset) at a later day at an agreed price. In return for granting the _____, the seller collects a payment (the premium) from the buyer. A call _____ gives the buyer the right to buy the underlying asset; a put _____ gives the buyer of the _____ the right to sell the underlying asset.

a. A4e
b. AAAI
c. A Stake in the Outcome
d. Option

36. _____ is a broad concept including proper prioritizing between career and ambition on one hand, compared with pleasure, leisure, family and spiritual development on the other.

As the separation between work and home life has diminished, this concept has become more relevant than ever before.

The expression was first used in the late 1970s to describe the balance between an individual's work and personal life.

a. Quality of working life
b. Workforce
c. Division of labour
d. Work-life balance

Chapter 12. Motivating Employees: Achieving Superior Performance in the Workplace 115

37. _____ is a variable work schedule, in contrast to traditional work arrangements requiring employees to work a standard 9am to 5pm day. Under _____, there is typically a core period of the day when employees are expected to be at work (for example, between 11 am and 3pm), while the rest of the working day is 'flexitime', in which employees can choose when they work, subject to achieving total daily, weekly or monthly hours in the region of what the employer expects, and subject to the necessary work being done.

A _____ policy allows staff to determine when they will work, while a flexplace policy allows staff to determine where they will work.

a. Fiduciary
b. Certificate of Incorporation
c. Bennett Amendment
d. Flextime

38. _____, e-commuting, e-work, telework, working from home (WFH), or working at home (WAH) is a work arrangement in which employees enjoy flexibility in working location and hours. In other words, the daily commute to a central place of work is replaced by telecommunication links. Many work from home, while others, occasionally also referred to as nomad workers or web commuters utilize mobile telecommunications technology to work from coffee shops or myriad other locations.

a. Telecommuting
b. 28-hour day
c. 33 Strategies of War
d. 1990 Clean Air Act

39. The legal _____ varies from nation to nation. The weekend is a part of the week usually lasting one or two days in which most paid workers do not work.

In Muslim-majority countries the legal work week in the Middle East is typically either Saturday through Wednesday , Saturday through Thursday or Sunday through Thursday as in Egypt.

a. Working Time Directive
b. Business day
c. Workweek
d. Day One Christian Ministries

40. _____ is an all encompassing term within a broad spectrum of post-secondary learning activities and programs. The term is used mainly in the United States. Recognized forms of post-secondary learning activities within the domain include: degree credit courses by non-traditional students, non-degree career training, workforce training, formal personal enrichment courses (both on-campus and online) self-directed learning (such as through Internet interest groups, clubs or personal research activities) and experiential learning as applied to problem solving.

a. 1990 Clean Air Act
b. 33 Strategies of War
c. 28-hour day
d. Continuing education

41. _____ is the provision of service to customers before, during and after a purchase.

According to Turban et al. (2002), '_____ is a series of activities designed to enhance the level of customer satisfaction - that is, the feeling that a product or service has met the customer expectation.'

Its importance varies by product, industry and customer; defective or broken merchandise can be exchanged, often only with a receipt and within a specified time frame.

Chapter 12. Motivating Employees: Achieving Superior Performance in the Workplace

a. Service rate
c. Customer service
b. 28-hour day
d. 1990 Clean Air Act

42. _____ is an advertisement in which a particular product specifically mentions a competitor by name for the express purpose of showing why the competitor is inferior to the product naming it.

This should not be confused with parody advertisements, where a fictional product is being advertised for the purpose of poking fun at the particular advertisement, nor should it be confused with the use of a coined brand name for the purpose of comparing the product without actually naming an actual competitor. ('Wikipedia tastes better and is less filling than the Encyclopedia Galactica.')

In the 1980s, during what has been referred to as the cola wars, soft-drink manufacturer Pepsi ran a series of advertisements where people, caught on hidden camera, in a blind taste test, chose Pepsi over rival Coca-Cola.

a. 28-hour day
c. 33 Strategies of War
b. Comparative advertising
d. 1990 Clean Air Act

Chapter 13. Groups & Teams: Increasing Cooperation, Reducing Conflict

1. The 'business case for _____', theorizes that in a global marketplace, a company that employs a diverse workforce (both men and women, people of many generations, people from ethnically and racially diverse backgrounds etc.) is better able to understand the demographics of the marketplace it serves and is thus better equipped to thrive in that marketplace than a company that has a more limited range of employee demographics.

An additional corollary suggests that a company that supports the _____ of its workforce can also improve employee satisfaction, productivity and retention.

   a. Virtual team
   b. Trademark
   c. Kanban
   d. Diversity

2. _____ is an idea in the field of Organizational studies and management which describes the psychology, attitudes, experiences, beliefs and Values (personal and cultural values) of an organization. It has been defined as 'the specific collection of values and norms that are shared by people and groups in an organization and that control the way they interact with each other and with stakeholders outside the organization.'

This definition continues to explain organizational values also known as 'beliefs and ideas about what kinds of goals members of an organization should pursue and ideas about the appropriate kinds or standards of behavior organizational members should use to achieve these goals. From organizational values develop organizational norms, guidelines or expectations that prescribe appropriate kinds of behavior by employees in particular situations and control the behavior of organizational members towards one another.'

_____ is not the same as corporate culture.

   a. Organizational culture
   b. Organizational effectiveness
   c. Organizational development
   d. Union shop

3. _____, e-commuting, e-work, telework, working from home (WFH), or working at home (WAH) is a work arrangement in which employees enjoy flexibility in working location and hours. In other words, the daily commute to a central place of work is replaced by telecommunication links. Many work from home, while others, occasionally also referred to as nomad workers or web commuters utilize mobile telecommunications technology to work from coffee shops or myriad other locations.
   a. 1990 Clean Air Act
   b. 33 Strategies of War
   c. Telecommuting
   d. 28-hour day

4. A _____ -- also known as a geographically dispersed team -- is a group of individuals who work across time, space, and organizational boundaries with links strengthened by webs of communication technology. They have complementary skills and are committed to a common purpose, have interdependent performance goals, and share an approach to work for which they hold themselves mutually accountable. Geographically dispersed teams allow organizations to hire and retain the best people regardless of location.
   a. Kanban
   b. Risk management
   c. Trademark
   d. Virtual team

Chapter 13. Groups & Teams: Increasing Cooperation, Reducing Conflict

5. _____ is one of the managerial functions like planning, organizing, staffing and directing. It is an important function because it helps to check the errors and to take the corrective action so that deviation from standards are minimized and stated goals of the organization are achieved in desired manner. According to modern concepts, _____ is a foreseeing action whereas earlier concept of _____ was used only when errors were detected. _____ in management means setting standards, measuring actual performance and taking corrective action.
   a. Turnover
   b. Schedule of reinforcement
   c. Decision tree pruning
   d. Control

6. _____ can be regarded as an outcome of mental processes (cognitive process) leading to the selection of a course of action among several alternatives. Every _____ process produces a final choice. The output can be an action or an opinion of choice.
   a. 1990 Clean Air Act
   b. Decision making
   c. 33 Strategies of War
   d. 28-hour day

7. In mathematics, a _____ law is (roughly speaking) a formal power series behaving as if it were the product of a Lie group. They were first defined in 1946 by S. Bochner. The term _____ sometimes means the same as _____ law, and sometimes means one of several generalizations.
   a. 28-hour day
   b. 1990 Clean Air Act
   c. 33 Strategies of War
   d. Formal group

8. _____ has been described as the 'process of social influence in which one person can enlist the aid and support of others in the accomplishment of a common task'. A definition more inclusive of followers comes from Alan Keith of Genentech who said '_____ is ultimately about creating a way for people to contribute to making something extraordinary happen.'

   _____ is one of the most salient aspects of the organizational context. However, defining _____ has been challenging.
   a. 28-hour day
   b. 1990 Clean Air Act
   c. Leadership
   d. Situational leadership

9. A _____ is a group of employees from various functional areas of the organization - research, engineering, marketing, finance. human resources, and operations, for example - who are all focused on a specific objective and are responsible to work as a team to improve coordination and innovation across divisions and resolve mutual problems.
   a. Sociotechnical systems
   b. Graduate recruitment
   c. Cross-functional team
   d. Goal-setting theory

10. A _____ is a volunteer group composed of workers (or even students), usually under the leadership of their supervisor (but they can elect a team leader), who are trained to identify, analyse and solve work-related problems and present their solutions to management in order to improve the performance of the organization, and motivate and enrich the work of employees. When matured, true _____s become self-managing, having gained the confidence of management.
    _____s are an alternative to the dehumanising concept of the Division of Labour, where workers or individuals are treated like robots.
    a. Competency-based job descriptions
    b. Quality circle
    c. Connectionist expert systems
    d. Certified in Production and Inventory Management

11. _____ refers to metrics and measures of output from production processes, per unit of input. Labor _____, for example, is typically measured as a ratio of output per labor-hour, an input. _____ may be conceived of as a metrics of the technical or engineering efficiency of production.
    a. Remanufacturing
    b. Master production schedule
    c. Value engineering
    d. Productivity

12. _____ refers to the movement of cash into or out of a business or financial product. It is usually measured during a specified, finite period of time. Measurement of _____ can be used

- to determine a project's rate of return or value. The time of _____s into and out of projects are used as inputs in financial models such as internal rate of return, and net present value.
- to determine problems with a business's liquidity. Being profitable does not necessarily mean being liquid. A company can fail because of a shortage of cash, even while profitable.
- as an alternate measure of a business's profits when it is believed that accrual accounting concepts do not represent economic realities. For example, a company may be notionally profitable but generating little operational cash (as may be the case for a company that barters its products rather than selling for cash.) In such a case, the company may be deriving additional operating cash by issuing shares evaluating default risk, re-investment requirements, etc.

_____ is a generic term used differently depending on the context. It may be defined by users for their own purposes.

    a. Gross profit
    b. Gross profit margin
    c. Sweat equity
    d. Cash flow

13. _____ is a concept in ethics with several meanings. It is often used synonymously with such concepts as responsibility, answerability, enforcement, blameworthiness, liability and other terms associated with the expectation of account-giving. As an aspect of governance, it has been central to discussions related to problems in both the public and private (corporation) worlds.
    a. A Stake in the Outcome
    b. Accountability
    c. Usury
    d. A4e

14. _____ describes the situation when output from (or information about the result of) an event or phenomenon in the past will influence the same event/phenomenon in the present or future. When an event is part of a chain of cause-and-effect that forms a circuit or loop, then the event is said to 'feed back' into itself.

_____ is also a synonym for:

- _____ signal; the information about the initial event that is the basis for subsequent modification of the event.
- _____ loop; the causal path that leads from the initial generation of the _____ signal to the subsequent modification of the event.

_____ is a mechanism, process or signal that is looped back to control a system within itself. Such a loop is called a _____ loop.

Chapter 13. Groups & Teams: Increasing Cooperation, Reducing Conflict

a. 1990 Clean Air Act
b. Feedback loop
c. Positive feedback
d. Feedback

15. In economics and sociology, an _____ is any factor (financial or non-financial) that enables or motivates a particular course of action, or counts as a reason for preferring one choice to the alternatives. It is an expectation that encourages people to behave in a certain way. Since human beings are purposeful creatures, the study of _____ structures is central to the study of all economic activity (both in terms of individual decision-making and in terms of co-operation and competition within a larger institutional structure.)
   a. A4e
   b. AAAI
   c. A Stake in the Outcome
   d. Incentive

16. In the social psychology of groups, _____ is the phenomenon of people making less effort to achieve a goal when they work in a group than when they work alone. This is seen as one of the main reasons groups are sometimes less productive than the combined performance of their members working as individuals.

   - Ringelmann, Max : 1913

   Research began in 1913 with Max Ringelmann's study. He found that when he asked a group of men to pull on a rope, that they did not pull as hard, or put as much effort into the activity, as they did when they were pulling alone.

   a. Self-enhancement
   b. Machiavellianism
   c. Personal space
   d. Social loafing

17. _____ is a type of thought exhibited by group members who try to minimize conflict and reach consensus without critically testing, analyzing, and evaluating ideas. Individual creativity, uniqueness, and independent thinking are lost in the pursuit of group cohesiveness, as are the advantages of reasonable balance in choice and thought that might normally be obtained by making decisions as a group. During _____, members of the group avoid promoting viewpoints outside the comfort zone of consensus thinking.
   a. Self-report inventory
   b. Diffusion of responsibility
   c. Psychological statistics
   d. Groupthink

18. _____ is complete agreement by everyone. When unanimous, everybody is of same mind and acting together as one. Many groups consider unanimous decisions a sign of agreement, solidarity, and unity.
   a. AAAI
   b. A Stake in the Outcome
   c. Unanimity
   d. A4e

19. _____ is a group creativity technique designed to generate a large number of ideas for the solution of a problem. The method was first popularized in the late 1930s by Alex Faickney Osborn in a book called Applied Imagination. Osborn proposed that groups could double their creative output with _____.
   a. Abraham Harold Maslow
   b. Adam Smith
   c. Affiliation
   d. Brainstorming

20. _____ is decision making in groups consisting of multiple members/entities. The challenge of group decision is deciding what action a group should take. There are various systems designed to solve this problem.

Chapter 13. Groups & Teams: Increasing Cooperation, Reducing Conflict

a. Groups Decision making
b. Genbutsu
c. Control of Substances Hazardous to Health Regulations 2002
d. Collaborative Planning, Forecasting and Replenishment

21. _____ is the act by an employer of terminating employment. Though such a decision can be made by an employer for a variety of reasons, ranging from an economic downturn to performance-related problems on the part of the employee, being fired has a strong stigma in many cultures. To be fired, as opposed to quitting voluntarily (or being laid off), is often perceived as being the employee's fault, and is therefore considered to be disgraceful and a sign of failure.

a. Severance package
b. Termination of employment
c. Layoff
d. Firing

22. _____ is a recursive process where two or more people or organizations work together in an intersection of common goals -- for example, an intellectual endeavor that is creative in nature--by sharing knowledge, learning and building consensus. _____ does not require leadership and can sometimes bring better results through decentralization and egalitarianism. In particular, teams that work collaboratively can obtain greater resources, recognition and reward when facing competition for finite resources. _____ is also present in opposing goals exhibiting the notion of adversarial _____, though this is not a common case for using the term.

a. 28-hour day
b. Collaboration
c. 1990 Clean Air Act
d. Collectivism

23. In game theory, an _____ is a set of moves or strategies taken by the players, or their payoffs resulting from the actions or strategies taken by all players. The two are complementary in that given knowledge of the set of strategies of all players, the final state of the game is known, as are any relevant payoffs. In a game where chance or a random event is involved, the _____ is not known from only the set of strategies, but is only realized when the random event(s) are realized.

a. A Stake in the Outcome
b. AAAI
c. A4e
d. Outcome

24. _____ is the pursuit of influencing outcomes -- including public-policy and resource allocation decisions within political, economic, and social systems and institutions -- that directly affect people's current lives. (Cohen, 2001)

Therefore, _____ can be seen as a deliberate process of speaking out on issues of concern in order to exert some influence on behalf of ideas or persons. Based on this definition, Cohen (2001) states that 'ideologues of all persuasions advocate' to bring a change in people's lives.

a. AAAI
b. Advocacy
c. A4e
d. A Stake in the Outcome

25. _____ is the strategic and coherent approach to the management of an organisation's most valued assets - the people working there who individually and collectively contribute to the achievement of the objectives of the business. The terms '_____' and 'human resources' (HR) have largely replaced the term 'personnel management' as a description of the processes involved in managing people in organizations. In simple sense, _____ means employing people, developing their resources, utilizing, maintaining and compensating their services in tune with the job and organizational requirement.

Chapter 13. Groups & Teams: Increasing Cooperation, Reducing Conflict

a. Job knowledge
b. Revolving door syndrome
c. Progressive discipline
d. Human resource management

26. _____ is a method by which the job performance of an employee is evaluated _____ is a part of career development.

_____s are regular reviews of employee performance within organizations

Generally, the aims of a _____ are to:

- Give feedback on performance to employees.
- Identify employee training needs.
- Document criteria used to allocate organizational rewards.
- Form a basis for personnel decisions: salary increases, promotions, disciplinary actions, etc.
- Provide the opportunity for organizational diagnosis and development.
- Facilitate communication between employee and administraton
- Validate selection techniques and human resource policies to meet federal Equal Employment Opportunity requirements.

A common approach to assessing performance is to use a numerical or scalar rating system whereby managers are asked to score an individual against a number of objectives/attributes. In some companies, employees receive assessments from their manager, peers, subordinates and customers while also performing a self assessment.

a. Progressive discipline
b. Personnel management
c. Human resource management
d. Performance appraisal

Chapter 14. Power, Influence, & Leadership: From Becoming a Manager to Becoming a Leader

1. _____ is a term defined by the Oxford English Dictionary as an individual's 'course or progress through life '. It is usually considered to pertain to remunerative work (and sometimes also formal education.)

The etymology of the term is somewhat ironic in that it comes from the Latin word carrera, which means race .

   a. Spatial mismatch   b. Career planning
   c. Career   d. Nursing shortage

2. _____ has been described as the 'process of social influence in which one person can enlist the aid and support of others in the accomplishment of a common task' . A definition more inclusive of followers comes from Alan Keith of Genentech who said '_____ is ultimately about creating a way for people to contribute to making something extraordinary happen.'

_____ is one of the most salient aspects of the organizational context. However, defining _____ has been challenging.

   a. 1990 Clean Air Act   b. Situational leadership
   c. Leadership   d. 28-hour day

3. _____ is an organization's process of defining its strategy and making decisions on allocating its resources to pursue this strategy, including its capital and people. Various business analysis techniques can be used in _____, including SWOT analysis (Strengths, Weaknesses, Opportunities, and Threats) and PEST analysis (Political, Economic, Social, and Technological analysis) or STEER analysis involving Socio-cultural, Technological, Economic, Ecological, and Regulatory factors and EPISTEL (Environment, Political, Informatic, Social, Technological, Economic and Legal)

_____ is the formal consideration of an organization's future course. All _____ deals with at least one of three key questions:

1. 'What do we do?'
2. 'For whom do we do it?'
3. 'How do we excel?'

In business _____, the third question is better phrased 'How can we beat or avoid competition?'. (Bradford and Duncan, page 1.)

   a. 28-hour day   b. 1990 Clean Air Act
   c. 33 Strategies of War   d. Strategic planning

4. _____ is one of the managerial functions like planning, organizing, staffing and directing. It is an important function because it helps to check the errors and to take the corrective action so that deviation from standards are minimized and stated goals of the organization are achieved in desired manner.According to modern concepts, _____ is a foreseeing action whereas earlier concept of _____ was used only when errors were detected. _____ in management means setting standards, measuring actual performance and taking corrective action.

   a. Decision tree pruning   b. Schedule of reinforcement
   c. Turnover   d. Control

Chapter 14. Power, Influence, & Leadership: From Becoming a Manager to Becoming a Leader

5. In economics and sociology, an _____ is any factor (financial or non-financial) that enables or motivates a particular course of action, or counts as a reason for preferring one choice to the alternatives. It is an expectation that encourages people to behave in a certain way. Since human beings are purposeful creatures, the study of _____ structures is central to the study of all economic activity (both in terms of individual decision-making and in terms of co-operation and competition within a larger institutional structure.)
   a. A4e
   b. AAAI
   c. A Stake in the Outcome
   d. Incentive

6. _____ refers to metrics and measures of output from production processes, per unit of input. Labor _____, for example, is typically measured as a ratio of output per labor-hour, an input. _____ may be conceived of as a metrics of the technical or engineering efficiency of production.
   a. Remanufacturing
   b. Value engineering
   c. Master production schedule
   d. Productivity

7. The _____ captures an expanded spectrum of values and criteria for measuring organizational success: economic, ecological and social. With the ratification of the United Nations and ICLEI _____ standard for urban and community accounting in early 2007, this became the dominant approach to public sector full cost accounting. Similar UN standards apply to natural capital and human capital measurement to assist in measurements required by _____, e.g. the ecoBudget standard for reporting ecological footprint.
   a. 28-hour day
   b. 1990 Clean Air Act
   c. Triple bottom line
   d. 33 Strategies of War

8. _____ is individual power based on a high level of identification with, admiration of, or respect for the powerholder. Nationalism, Patriotism, Celebrities and well-respected people are examples of _____ in effect.

_____ is one of the Five Bases of Social Power, as defined by Bertram Raven and his colleagues[1] in 1959.

   a. Referent power
   b. 33 Strategies of War
   c. 28-hour day
   d. 1990 Clean Air Act

9. _____ is an emerging movement to explicitly use the current, best evidence in management decision-making. Its roots are in evidence-based medicine, a quality movement to apply the scientific method to medical practice.

_____ entails managerial decisions and organizational practices informed by the best available scientific evidence.

   a. Evidence-based management
   b. Enterprise Decision Management
   c. Anti-leadership
   d. Entrenchment Management

10. _____ is a form of social influence. It is the process of guiding people and oneself toward the adoption of an idea, attitude, or action by rational and symbolic (though not always logical) means. It is strategy of problem-solving relying on 'appeals' rather than coercion.
    a. Persuasion
    b. Personal space
    c. Self-enhancement
    d. Social loafing

Chapter 14. Power, Influence, & Leadership: From Becoming a Manager to Becoming a Leader

11. A _____ is an alliance among individuals or groups, during which they cooperate in joint action, each in his own self-interest, joining forces together for a common cause. This alliance may be temporary or a matter of convenience. A _____ thus differs from a more formal covenant.

- a. 28-hour day
- b. 33 Strategies of War
- c. 1990 Clean Air Act
- d. Coalition

12. _____ of the learning curve effect and the closely related experience curve effect express the relationship between equations for experience and efficiency or between efficiency gains and investment in the effort. The experience of 'learning curves' was first observed by the 19th Century German psychologist Hermann Ebbinghaus according to the difficulty of memorizing varying numbers of verbal stimuli, and subsequent learning about the complex processes of learning are discussed in the

.

The rule used for representing the learning curve effect states that the more times a task has been performed, the less time will be required on each subsequent iteration.

- a. Distribution
- b. Spatial Decision Support Systems
- c. Point biserial correlation coefficient
- d. Models

13. _____ refers to the movement of cash into or out of a business or financial product. It is usually measured during a specified, finite period of time. Measurement of _____ can be used

- to determine a project's rate of return or value. The time of _____s into and out of projects are used as inputs in financial models such as internal rate of return, and net present value.
- to determine problems with a business's liquidity. Being profitable does not necessarily mean being liquid. A company can fail because of a shortage of cash, even while profitable.
- as an alternate measure of a business's profits when it is believed that accrual accounting concepts do not represent economic realities. For example, a company may be notionally profitable but generating little operational cash (as may be the case for a company that barters its products rather than selling for cash.) In such a case, the company may be deriving additional operating cash by issuing shares evaluating default risk, re-investment requirements, etc.

_____ is a generic term used differently depending on the context. It may be defined by users for their own purposes.

- a. Gross profit
- b. Sweat equity
- c. Gross profit margin
- d. Cash flow

14. _____ and benefits in kind are various non-wage compensations provided to employees in addition to their normal wages or salaries. Where an employee exchanges (cash) wages for some other form of benefit, this is generally referred to as a 'salary sacrifice' arrangement. In most countries, most kinds of _____ are taxable to at least some degree.

- a. Interactive Accommodation Process
- b. A Stake in the Outcome
- c. Employee benefits
- d. A4e

Chapter 14. Power, Influence, & Leadership: From Becoming a Manager to Becoming a Leader

15. _____ is subcontracting a process, such as product design or manufacturing, to a third-party company. The decision to outsource is often made in the interest of lowering cost or making better use of time and energy costs, redirecting or conserving energy directed at the competencies of a particular business, or to make more efficient use of land, labor, capital, (information) technology and resources. _____ became part of the business lexicon during the 1980s.
   - a. Operant conditioning
   - b. Opinion leadership
   - c. Unemployment insurance
   - d. Outsourcing

16. _____ is a term in psychology which refers to a person's belief about what causes the good or bad results in his or her life, either in general or in a specific area such as health or academics. Understanding of the concept was developed by Julian B. Rotter in 1954, and has since become an important aspect of personality studies.

   _____ refers to the extent to which individuals believe that they can control events that affect them.

   - a. Social loafing
   - b. Self-enhancement
   - c. Machiavellianism
   - d. Locus of control

17. _____ can be regarded as an outcome of mental processes (cognitive process) leading to the selection of a course of action among several alternatives. Every _____ process produces a final choice. The output can be an action or an opinion of choice.
   - a. Decision making
   - b. 1990 Clean Air Act
   - c. 33 Strategies of War
   - d. 28-hour day

18. The _____, is a situational leadership theory developed by Paul Hersey, a professor who wrote a well known book 'Situational Leader' and Ken Blanchard, the management guru who later became famous for his 'One Minute Manager' series. They created a model of situational leadership in the late 1960s in their work Management of Organizational Behavior (now in its 9th edition) that allows one to analyze the needs of the situation, then adopt the most appropriate leadership style. It has been proven popular with managers over the years because it is simple to understand, and it works in most environments for most people.
   - a. Hersey-Blanchard situational theory
   - b. Goal-setting theory
   - c. Cross-functional team
   - d. Human relations

19. Contingency leadership theory in organizational studies is a type of leadership theory, leadership style, and leadership model that presumes that different leadership styles are contingent to different situations. It is also referred as _____ ® theory although, as originally convened, the situational theory term is much more restrictive. The original situational theory argues that the best type of leadership is totally determined by the situational variables. Currently there are many styles of leadership.
   - a. 1990 Clean Air Act
   - b. Situational theory
   - c. Situational leadership
   - d. 28-hour day

20. Contingency leadership theory in organizational studies is a type of leadership theory, leadership style, and leadership model that presumes that different leadership styles are contingent to different situations. It is also referred as Situational Leadership^® theory although, as originally convened, the _____ term is much more restrictive. The original _____ argues that the best type of leadership is totally determined by the situational variables. Currently there are many styles of leadership.

Chapter 14. Power, Influence, & Leadership: From Becoming a Manager to Becoming a Leader

   a. 1990 Clean Air Act
   b. 28-hour day
   c. Situational leadership
   d. Situational theory

21. _____ is a term used to classify a group leadership theories that inquire the interactions between leaders and followers. A transactional leader focuses more on a series of 'transactions'. This person is interested in looking out for oneself, having exchange benefits with their subordinates and clarify a sense of duty with rewards and punishments to reach goals.
   a. 33 Strategies of War
   b. 28-hour day
   c. Transactional leadership
   d. 1990 Clean Air Act

22. _____ is a leadership style that defines as leadership that creates voluble and positive change in the followers. A transformational leader focuses on 'transforming' others to help each other, to look out for each other, be encouraging, harmonious, and look out for the organization as a whole. In this leadership, the leader enhances the motivation, moral and performance of his follower group.
   a. SESAMO
   b. Strong-Campbell Interest Inventory
   c. Polynomial conjoint measurement
   d. Transformational leadership

23. _____ is an approach to leadership development, coined and defined by Robert Greenleaf and advanced by several authors such as Stephen Covey, Peter Block, Peter Senge, Max DePree, Margaret Wheatley, Ken Blanchard, and others. Servant-leadership emphasizes the leader's role as steward of the resources (human, financial and otherwise) provided by the organization. It encourages leaders to serve others while staying focused on achieving results in line with the organization's values and integrity.
   a. Adam Smith
   b. Affiliation
   c. Abraham Harold Maslow
   d. Servant leadership

Chapter 15. Interpersonal & Organizational Communication

1. _____ describes the situation when output from (or information about the result of) an event or phenomenon in the past will influence the same event/phenomenon in the present or future. When an event is part of a chain of cause-and-effect that forms a circuit or loop, then the event is said to 'feed back' into itself.

_____ is also a synonym for:

- _____ signal; the information about the initial event that is the basis for subsequent modification of the event.
- _____ loop; the causal path that leads from the initial generation of the _____ signal to the subsequent modification of the event.

_____ is a mechanism, process or signal that is looped back to control a system within itself. Such a loop is called a _____ loop.

a. 1990 Clean Air Act
c. Positive feedback
b. Feedback loop
d. Feedback

2. _____ is a field of study that looks at how people from differing cultural backgrounds endeavour to communicate.

In years during and preceding the Cold War, the United States economy was largely self-contained because the world was polarized into two separate and competing powers: the east and west. However, changes and advancements in economic relationships, political systems, and technological options began to break down old cultural barriers.

a. 1990 Clean Air Act
c. 33 Strategies of War
b. 28-hour day
d. Cross-cultural communication

3. The 'business case for _____', theorizes that in a global marketplace, a company that employs a diverse workforce (both men and women, people of many generations, people from ethnically and racially diverse backgrounds etc.) is better able to understand the demographics of the marketplace it serves and is thus better equipped to thrive in that marketplace than a company that has a more limited range of employee demographics.

An additional corollary suggests that a company that supports the _____ of its workforce can also improve employee satisfaction, productivity and retention.

a. Virtual team
c. Trademark
b. Kanban
d. Diversity

4. _____ is an idea in the field of Organizational studies and management which describes the psychology, attitudes, experiences, beliefs and Values (personal and cultural values) of an organization. It has been defined as 'the specific collection of values and norms that are shared by people and groups in an organization and that control the way they interact with each other and with stakeholders outside the organization.'

Chapter 15. Interpersonal & Organizational Communication

This definition continues to explain organizational values also known as 'beliefs and ideas about what kinds of goals members of an organization should pursue and ideas about the appropriate kinds or standards of behavior organizational members should use to achieve these goals. From organizational values develop organizational norms, guidelines or expectations that prescribe appropriate kinds of behavior by employees in particular situations and control the behavior of organizational members towards one another.'

_____ is not the same as corporate culture.

a. Organizational development
b. Union shop
c. Organizational effectiveness
d. Organizational culture

5. _____ is a term defined by the Oxford English Dictionary as an individual's 'course or progress through life '. It is usually considered to pertain to remunerative work (and sometimes also formal education.)

The etymology of the term is somewhat ironic in that it comes from the Latin word carrera, which means race .

a. Career planning
b. Nursing shortage
c. Spatial mismatch
d. Career

6. In a military context, the _____ is the line of authority and responsibility along which orders are passed within a military unit and between different units. The term is also used in a civilian management context describing comparable hierarchical structures of authority.

a. 1990 Clean Air Act
b. 28-hour day
c. Chain of command
d. French leave

7. An _____ is a mostly hierarchical concept of subordination of entities that collaborate and contribute to serve one common aim.

Organizations are a variant of clustered entities. The structure of an organization is usually set up in many a styles, dependent on their objectives and ambience.

a. Informal organization
b. Organizational development
c. Organizational structure
d. Open shop

8. _____ is a method by which the job performance of an employee is evaluated _____ is a part of career development.

_____s are regular reviews of employee performance within organizations

Generally, the aims of a _____ are to:

- Give feedback on performance to employees.
- Identify employee training needs.
- Document criteria used to allocate organizational rewards.
- Form a basis for personnel decisions: salary increases, promotions, disciplinary actions, etc.
- Provide the opportunity for organizational diagnosis and development.
- Facilitate communication between employee and administraton
- Validate selection techniques and human resource policies to meet federal Equal Employment Opportunity requirements.

A common approach to assessing performance is to use a numerical or scalar rating system whereby managers are asked to score an individual against a number of objectives/attributes. In some companies, employees receive assessments from their manager, peers, subordinates and customers while also performing a self assessment.

a. Performance appraisal
b. Personnel management
c. Human resource management
d. Progressive discipline

9. An _____ is a private computer network that uses Internet technologies to securely share any part of an organization's information or operational systems with its employees. Sometimes the term refers only to the organization's internal website, but often it is a more extensive part of the organization's computer infrastructure and private websites are an important component and focal point of internal communication and collaboration.

An _____ is built from the same concepts and technologies used for the Internet, such as client-server computing and the Internet Protocol Suite (TCP/IP.)

a. A Stake in the Outcome
b. AAAI
c. A4e
d. Intranet

10. An _____ is a private network that uses Internet protocols, network connectivity, and possibly the public telecommunication system to securely share part of an organization's information or operations with suppliers, vendors, partners, customers or other businesses. An _____ can be viewed as part of a company's intranet that is extended to users outside the company (e.g.: normally over the Internet.) It has also been described as a 'state of mind' in which the Internet is perceived as a way to do business with a preapproved set of other companies business-to-business (B2B), in isolation from all other Internet users.

a. A4e
b. AAAI
c. A Stake in the Outcome
d. Extranet

11. _____, e-commuting, e-work, telework, working from home (WFH), or working at home (WAH) is a work arrangement in which employees enjoy flexibility in working location and hours. In other words, the daily commute to a central place of work is replaced by telecommunication links. Many work from home, while others, occasionally also referred to as nomad workers or web commuters utilize mobile telecommunications technology to work from coffee shops or myriad other locations.

Chapter 15. Interpersonal & Organizational Communication

a. 28-hour day
b. 1990 Clean Air Act
c. 33 Strategies of War
d. Telecommuting

12. A _____ -- also known as a geographically dispersed team -- is a group of individuals who work across time, space, and organizational boundaries with links strengthened by webs of communication technology. They have complementary skills and are committed to a common purpose, have interdependent performance goals, and share an approach to work for which they hold themselves mutually accountable. Geographically dispersed teams allow organizations to hire and retain the best people regardless of location.

a. Trademark
b. Kanban
c. Virtual team
d. Risk management

13. The _____ is a form of reactivity whereby subjects improve an aspect of their behavior being experimentally measured simply in response to the fact that they are being studied, not in response to any particular experimental manipulation.

The term was coined in 1955 by Henry A. Landsberger when analyzing older experiments from 1924-1932 at the Hawthorne Works (outside Chicago.) Hawthorne Works had commissioned a study to see if its workers would become more productive in higher or lower levels of light.

a. 1990 Clean Air Act
b. Hawthorne effect
c. 33 Strategies of War
d. 28-hour day

14. _____ is an integrated communications-based process through which individuals and communities discover that existing and newly-identified needs and wants may be satisfied by the products and services of others.

_____ is defined by the American _____ Association as the activity, set of institutions, and processes for creating, communicating, delivering, and exchanging offerings that have value for customers, clients, partners, and society at large. The term developed from the original meaning which referred literally to going to market, as in shopping, or going to a market to buy or sell goods or services.

a. Market development
b. Marketing
c. Customer relationship management
d. Disruptive technology

15. A _____ is a process that can allow an organization to concentrate its limited resources on the greatest opportunities to increase sales and achieve a sustainable competitive advantage. A _____ should be centered around the key concept that customer satisfaction is the main goal.

A _____ is a written plan which combines product development, promotion, distribution, and pricing approach, identifies the firm's marketing goals, and explains how they will be achieved within a stated timeframe.

a. Marketing strategy
b. Disruptive technology
c. Category management
d. Product bundling

16. _____ refers to metrics and measures of output from production processes, per unit of input. Labor _____, for example, is typically measured as a ratio of output per labor-hour, an input. _____ may be conceived of as a metrics of the technical or engineering efficiency of production.

a. Master production schedule
b. Productivity
c. Value engineering
d. Remanufacturing

17. _____ is the strategic and coherent approach to the management of an organisation's most valued assets - the people working there who individually and collectively contribute to the achievement of the objectives of the business. The terms '_____' and 'human resources' (HR) have largely replaced the term 'personnel management' as a description of the processes involved in managing people in organizations. In simple sense, _____ means employing people, developing their resources, utilizing, maintaining and compensating their services in tune with the job and organizational requirement.

a. Job knowledge
b. Revolving door syndrome
c. Progressive discipline
d. Human resource management

Chapter 16. Control: Techniques for Enhancing Organizational Effectiveness 133

1. The 'business case for _____', theorizes that in a global marketplace, a company that employs a diverse workforce (both men and women, people of many generations, people from ethnically and racially diverse backgrounds etc.) is better able to understand the demographics of the marketplace it serves and is thus better equipped to thrive in that marketplace than a company that has a more limited range of employee demographics.

An additional corollary suggests that a company that supports the _____ of its workforce can also improve employee satisfaction, productivity and retention.

    a. Trademark   b. Diversity
    c. Virtual team   d. Kanban

2. The _____ is a form of reactivity whereby subjects improve an aspect of their behavior being experimentally measured simply in response to the fact that they are being studied, not in response to any particular experimental manipulation.

The term was coined in 1955 by Henry A. Landsberger when analyzing older experiments from 1924-1932 at the Hawthorne Works (outside Chicago.) Hawthorne Works had commissioned a study to see if its workers would become more productive in higher or lower levels of light.

    a. 33 Strategies of War   b. 28-hour day
    c. 1990 Clean Air Act   d. Hawthorne effect

3. _____ is the strategic and coherent approach to the management of an organisation's most valued assets - the people working there who individually and collectively contribute to the achievement of the objectives of the business. The terms '_____' and 'human resources' (HR) have largely replaced the term 'personnel management' as a description of the processes involved in managing people in organizations. In simple sense, _____ means employing people, developing their resources, utilizing, maintaining and compensating their services in tune with the job and organizational requirement.

    a. Progressive discipline   b. Revolving door syndrome
    c. Human resource management   d. Job knowledge

4. The phrase _____, according to the Organization for Economic Co-operation and Development, refers to 'creative work undertaken on a systematic basis in order to increase the stock of knowledge, including knowledge of man, culture and society, and the use of this stock of knowledge to devise new applications [sic]'

New product design and development is more than often a crucial factor in the survival of a company. In an industry that is fast changing, firms must continually revise their design and range of products. This is necessary due to continuous technology change and development as well as other competitors and the changing preference of customers.

    a. 33 Strategies of War   b. 1990 Clean Air Act
    c. 28-hour day   d. Research and development

5. _____ is a term defined by the Oxford English Dictionary as an individual's 'course or progress through life '. It is usually considered to pertain to remunerative work (and sometimes also formal education.)

The etymology of the term is somewhat ironic in that it comes from the Latin word carrera, which means race .

a. Career
b. Spatial mismatch
c. Nursing shortage
d. Career planning

6. _____ is one of the managerial functions like planning, organizing, staffing and directing. It is an important function because it helps to check the errors and to take the corrective action so that deviation from standards are minimized and stated goals of the organization are achieved in desired manner. According to modern concepts, _____ is a foreseeing action whereas earlier concept of _____ was used only when errors were detected. _____ in management means setting standards, measuring actual performance and taking corrective action.
   a. Schedule of reinforcement
   b. Control
   c. Turnover
   d. Decision tree pruning

7. In economics and sociology, an _____ is any factor (financial or non-financial) that enables or motivates a particular course of action, or counts as a reason for preferring one choice to the alternatives. It is an expectation that encourages people to behave in a certain way. Since human beings are purposeful creatures, the study of _____ structures is central to the study of all economic activity (both in terms of individual decision-making and in terms of co-operation and competition within a larger institutional structure.)
   a. AAAI
   b. A4e
   c. A Stake in the Outcome
   d. Incentive

8. In statistics, _____ is:

   - the arithmetic _____
   - the expected value of a random variable, which is also called the population _____.

It is sometimes stated that the '_____' _____s average. This is incorrect if '_____' is taken in the specific sense of 'arithmetic _____' as there are different types of averages: the _____, median, and mode. Other simple statistical analyses use measures of spread, such as range, interquartile range, or standard deviation. For a real-valued random variable X, the _____ is the expectation of X. Note that not every probability distribution has a defined _____; see the Cauchy distribution for an example.

   a. Statistical inference
   b. Correlation
   c. Control chart
   d. Mean

9. _____ refers to metrics and measures of output from production processes, per unit of input. Labor _____, for example, is typically measured as a ratio of output per labor-hour, an input. _____ may be conceived of as a metrics of the technical or engineering efficiency of production.
   a. Master production schedule
   b. Value engineering
   c. Remanufacturing
   d. Productivity

10. _____ is the amount of goods and services that a labourer produces in a given amount of time. It is one of several types of productivity that economists measure. _____ can be measured for a firm, a process or a country.
    a. Business Network Transformation
    b. Time and attendance
    c. Retroactive overtime
    d. Labour productivity

11. _____ is an advertisement in which a particular product specifically mentions a competitor by name for the express purpose of showing why the competitor is inferior to the product naming it.

Chapter 16. Control: Techniques for Enhancing Organizational Effectiveness

This should not be confused with parody advertisements, where a fictional product is being advertised for the purpose of poking fun at the particular advertisement, nor should it be confused with the use of a coined brand name for the purpose of comparing the product without actually naming an actual competitor. ('Wikipedia tastes better and is less filling than the Encyclopedia Galactica.')

In the 1980s, during what has been referred to as the cola wars, soft-drink manufacturer Pepsi ran a series of advertisements where people, caught on hidden camera, in a blind taste test, chose Pepsi over rival Coca-Cola.

- a. 1990 Clean Air Act
- b. 28-hour day
- c. 33 Strategies of War
- d. Comparative advertising

12. _____ is subcontracting a process, such as product design or manufacturing, to a third-party company. The decision to outsource is often made in the interest of lowering cost or making better use of time and energy costs, redirecting or conserving energy directed at the competencies of a particular business, or to make more efficient use of land, labor, capital, (information) technology and resources. _____ became part of the business lexicon during the 1980s.

- a. Unemployment insurance
- b. Operant conditioning
- c. Opinion leadership
- d. Outsourcing

13. The term '_____' refers to the concept of collecting information and attempting to spot a pattern in the information. In some fields of study, the term '_____' has more formally-defined meanings.

In project management _____ is a mathematical technique that uses historical results to predict future outcome.

- a. Regression analysis
- b. Least squares
- c. Trend analysis
- d. Stepwise regression

14. _____ is an organization's process of defining its strategy and making decisions on allocating its resources to pursue this strategy, including its capital and people. Various business analysis techniques can be used in _____, including SWOT analysis (Strengths, Weaknesses, Opportunities, and Threats) and PEST analysis (Political, Economic, Social, and Technological analysis) or STEER analysis involving Socio-cultural, Technological, Economic, Ecological, and Regulatory factors and EPISTEL (Environment, Political, Informatic, Social, Technological, Economic and Legal)

_____ is the formal consideration of an organization's future course. All _____ deals with at least one of three key questions:

1. 'What do we do?'
2. 'For whom do we do it?'
3. 'How do we excel?'

In business _____, the third question is better phrased 'How can we beat or avoid competition?'. (Bradford and Duncan, page 1.)

a. 28-hour day
b. 33 Strategies of War
c. 1990 Clean Air Act
d. Strategic planning

15. A _____ is a list of the general tasks and responsibilities of a position. Typically, it also includes to whom the position reports, specifications such as the qualifications needed by the person in the job, salary range for the position, etc. A _____ is usually developed by conducting a job analysis, which includes examining the tasks and sequences of tasks necessary to perform the job.
  a. Job description
  b. Recruitment advertising
  c. Recruitment
  d. Recruitment Process Insourcing

16. In economics, business, retail, and accounting, a _____ is the value of money that has been used up to produce something, and hence is not available for use anymore. In economics, a _____ is an alternative that is given up as a result of a decision. In business, the _____ may be one of acquisition, in which case the amount of money expended to acquire it is counted as _____.
  a. Fixed costs
  b. Cost
  c. Cost overrun
  d. Cost allocation

17. _____ is the process whereby companies use cost accounting to report or control the various costs of doing business.

_____ generally describes the approaches and activities of managers in short run and long run planning and control decisions that increase value for customers and lower costs of products and services.

  a. Missing completely at random
  b. Strict liability
  c. Genbutsu
  d. Cost Management

18. In engineering and manufacturing, _____ and quality engineering are used in developing systems to ensure products or services are designed and produced to meet or exceed customer requirements. Refer to the definition by Merriam-Webster for further information . These systems are often developed in conjunction with other business and engineering disciplines using a cross-functional approach.
  a. Process capability
  b. Single Minute Exchange of Die
  c. Statistical process control
  d. Quality control

19. _____ can be regarded as an outcome of mental processes (cognitive process) leading to the selection of a course of action among several alternatives. Every _____ process produces a final choice. The output can be an action or an opinion of choice.
  a. 28-hour day
  b. 33 Strategies of War
  c. 1990 Clean Air Act
  d. Decision making

20. A _____ is a change implemented to address a weakness identified in a management system. Normally _____s are implemented in response to a customer complaint, abnormal levels of internal nonconformity, nonconformities identified during an internal audit or adverse or unstable trends in product and process monitoring such as would be identified by SPC.

The process of determining a _____ requires identification of actions that can be taken to prevent or mitigate the weakness.

Chapter 16. Control: Techniques for Enhancing Organizational Effectiveness

a. 28-hour day
b. 1990 Clean Air Act
c. Zero defects
d. Corrective action

21. _____ is a 'policy by which management devotes its time to investigating only those situations in which actual results differ significantly from planned results. The idea is that management should spend its valuable time concentrating on the more important items (such as shaping the company's future strategic course.) Attention is given only to material deviations requiring investigation.'

It is not entirely synonymous with the concept of exception management in that it describes a policy where absolute focus is on exception management, in contrast to moderate application of exception management.

a. C-A-K-E
b. Trustee
c. Business philosophy
d. Management by exception

22. The _____ is a performance management tool for measuring whether the smaller-scale operational activities of a company are aligned with its larger-scale objectives in terms of vision and strategy.

By focusing not only on financial outcomes but also on the operational, marketing and developmental inputs to these, the _____ helps provide a more comprehensive view of a business, which in turn helps organizations act in their best long-term interests. This tool is also being used to address business response to climate change and greenhouse gas emissions.

a. Management development
b. Commercial management
c. Middle management
d. Balanced scorecard

23. A _____ or chief executive is one of the highest-ranking corporate officer (executive) or administrator in charge of total management. An individual selected as President and _____ of a corporation, company, organization, or agency, reports to the board of directors. In internal communication and press releases, many companies capitalize the term and those of other high positions, even when they are not proper nouns.

a. Chief brand officer
b. Financial analyst
c. Purchasing manager
d. Chief executive officer

24. _____ is an emerging movement to explicitly use the current, best evidence in management decision-making. Its roots are in evidence-based medicine, a quality movement to apply the scientific method to medical practice.

_____ entails managerial decisions and organizational practices informed by the best available scientific evidence.

a. Entrenchment Management
b. Evidence-based management
c. Anti-leadership
d. Enterprise Decision Management

25. While _____ literally refers to a person responsible for the performance of duties involved in running an organization, the exact meaning of the role is variable, depending on the organization.

While there is no clear line between executive or principal and inferior officers, principal officers are high-level officials in the executive branch of U.S. government such as department heads of independent agencies. In Humphrey's Executor v. United States, 295 U.S. 602 (1935), the Court distinguished between _____s and quasi-legislative or quasi-judicial officers by stating that the former serve at the pleasure of the President and may be removed at his discretion.

a. Australian Fair Pay and Conditions Standard
b. Easement
c. Unreported employment
d. Executive officer

26. _____ is the provision of service to customers before, during and after a purchase.

According to Turban et al. (2002), '_____ is a series of activities designed to enhance the level of customer satisfaction - that is, the feeling that a product or service has met the customer expectation.'

Its importance varies by product, industry and customer; defective or broken merchandise can be exchanged, often only with a receipt and within a specified time frame.

a. Customer service
b. 28-hour day
c. 1990 Clean Air Act
d. Service rate

27. A _____ is a process in which a potential employee is evaluated by an employer for prospective employment in their company, organization and was established in the late 16th century.

A _____ typically precedes the hiring decision, and is used to evaluate the candidate. The interview is usually preceded by the evaluation of submitted résumés from interested candidates, then selecting a small number of candidates for interviews.

a. Payrolling
b. Split shift
c. Supported employment
d. Job interview

28. _____ is a method by which the job performance of an employee is evaluated _____ is a part of career development.

_____s are regular reviews of employee performance within organizations

Chapter 16. Control: Techniques for Enhancing Organizational Effectiveness

Generally, the aims of a _____ are to:

- Give feedback on performance to employees.
- Identify employee training needs.
- Document criteria used to allocate organizational rewards.
- Form a basis for personnel decisions: salary increases, promotions, disciplinary actions, etc.
- Provide the opportunity for organizational diagnosis and development.
- Facilitate communication between employee and administraton
- Validate selection techniques and human resource policies to meet federal Equal Employment Opportunity requirements.

A common approach to assessing performance is to use a numerical or scalar rating system whereby managers are asked to score an individual against a number of objectives/attributes. In some companies, employees receive assessments from their manager, peers, subordinates and customers while also performing a self assessment.

a. Progressive discipline
c. Human resource management
b. Personnel management
d. Performance appraisal

29. In decision theory and estimation theory, the _____ of an estimator, $\hat{\theta}$, of an unknown parameter of the distribution, θ, is the expected value of the loss function

$$R(\theta, \hat{\theta}) = \mathbb{E}_\theta L(\theta, \hat{\theta}) = \int L(\theta, \hat{\theta}) \, dP_\theta.$$

where dP_θ is a probability measure parametrized by θ.

- For a scalar parameter θ and a quadratic loss function,

$$L(\theta, \hat{\theta}) = (\theta - \hat{\theta})^2$$

 the _____ function becomes the mean squared error of the estimate,

$$R(\theta, \hat{\theta}) = E_\theta (\theta - \hat{\theta})^2$$

- In density estimation, the unknown parameter is probability density itself. The loss function is typically chosen to be a norm in an appropriate function space. For example, for L^2 norm,

$$L(f, \hat{f}) = \|f - \hat{f}\|_2^2$$

 the _____ function becomes the mean integrated squared error

$$R(f, \hat{f}) = E\|f - \hat{f}\|^2$$

a. Financial modeling
c. Linear model
b. Risk
d. Risk aversion

30. The inverse of a person's risk aversion is sometimes called their _____

A person is given the choice between two scenarios, one with a guaranteed payoff and one without. In the guaranteed scenario, the person receives $50. In the uncertain scenario, a coin is flipped to decide whether the person receives $100 or nothing. The expected payoff for both scenarios is $50, meaning that an individual who was insensitive to risk would not care whether they took the guaranteed payment or the gamble.

a. Discounting
c. Risk
b. Ruin theory
d. Risk tolerance

31. _____ is a structured approach to transitioning individuals, teams, and organizations from a current state to a desired future state. The current definition of _____ includes both organizational _____ processes and individual _____ models, which together are used to manage the people side of change.

A number of models are available for understanding the transitioning of individuals through the phases of _____ and strengthening organizational development initiative in both government and corporate sectors.

Chapter 16. Control: Techniques for Enhancing Organizational Effectiveness

    a. 33 Strategies of War
    b. 28-hour day
    c. Change management
    d. 1990 Clean Air Act

32. Engineering _____ is the permissible limit of variation in

   1. a physical dimension,
   2. a measured value or physical property of a material, manufactured object, system, or service,
   3. other measured values (such as temperature, humidity, etc.)
   4. in engineering and safety, a physical distance or space (_____), as in a truck (lorry), train or boat under a bridge as well as a train in a tunnel

Dimensions, properties, or conditions may vary within certain practical limits without significantly affecting functioning of equipment or a process. _____s are specified to allow reasonable leeway for imperfections and inherent variability without compromising performance.

The _____ may be specified as a factor or percentage of the nominal value, a maximum deviation from a nominal value, an explicit range of allowed values, be specified by a note or published standard with this information, or be implied by the numeric accuracy of the nominal value. _____ can be symmetrical, as in 40±0.1, or asymmetrical, such as 40+0.2/−0.1.

    a. Tolerance
    b. Zero defects
    c. Quality assurance
    d. Root cause analysis

33. _____ generally refers to a list of all planned expenses and revenues. It is a plan for saving and spending. A _____ is an important concept in microeconomics, which uses a _____ line to illustrate the trade-offs between two or more goods.

    a. Budget
    b. 1990 Clean Air Act
    c. 28-hour day
    d. 33 Strategies of War

34. _____ is a technique of planning and decision-making which reverses the working process of traditional budgeting. In traditional incremental budgeting, departmental managers justify only increases over the previous year budget and what has been already spent is automatically sanctioned. No reference is made to the previous level of expenditure.

    a. 1990 Clean Air Act
    b. Zero-based budgeting
    c. 33 Strategies of War
    d. 28-hour day

35. _____s (CAPEX or capex) are expenditures creating future benefits. A _____ is incurred when a business spends money either to buy fixed assets or to add to the value of an existing fixed asset with a useful life that extends beyond the taxable year. Capex are used by a company to acquire or upgrade physical assets such as equipment, property, or industrial buildings.

    a. Weighted average cost of capital
    b. Capital intensive
    c. 1990 Clean Air Act
    d. Capital expenditure

36. An _____ is the annual budget of an activity stated in terms of Budget Classification Code, functional/subfunctional categories and cost accounts. It contains estimates of the total value of resources required for the performance of the operation including reimbursable work or services for others. It also includes estimates of workload in terms of total work units identified by cost accounts.

Chapter 16. Control: Techniques for Enhancing Organizational Effectiveness

a. Operating budget
b. Expected gain
c. Inflation rate
d. Expected return

37. In business and accounting, _____s are everything of value that is owned by a person or company. Any property or object of value that one possesses, usually considered as applicable to the payment of one's debts is considered an _____. Simplistically stated, _____s are things of value that can be readily converted into cash.

a. A Stake in the Outcome
b. AAAI
c. A4e
d. Asset

38. The general definition of an _____ is an evaluation of a person, organization, system, process, project or product. _____s are performed to ascertain the validity and reliability of information; also to provide an assessment of a system's internal control. The goal of an _____ is to express an opinion on the person / organization/system (etc) in question, under evaluation based on work done on a test basis.

a. Audit committee
b. A Stake in the Outcome
c. Internal control
d. Audit

39. In financial accounting, a _____ or statement of financial position is a summary of a person's or organization's balances. Assets, liabilities and ownership equity are listed as of a specific date, such as the end of its financial year. A _____ is often described as a snapshot of a company's financial condition.

a. 1990 Clean Air Act
b. Balance sheet
c. 33 Strategies of War
d. 28-hour day

40. In accounting, a _____ is an asset on the balance sheet which is expected to be sold or otherwise used up in the near future, usually within one year, or one business cycle - whichever is longer. Typical _____s include cash, cash equivalents, accounts receivable, inventory, the portion of prepaid accounts which will be used within a year, and short-term investments.

On the balance sheet, assets will typically be classified into _____s and long-term assets.

a. Net income
b. Current asset
c. Matching principle
d. Treasury stock

41. _____ are formal records of the financial activities of a business, person, or other entity. In British English, including United Kingdom company law, _____ are often referred to as accounts, although the term _____ is also used, particularly by accountants.

_____ provide an overview of a business or person's financial condition in both short and long term.

a. Financial statements
b. 33 Strategies of War
c. 1990 Clean Air Act
d. 28-hour day

42. _____ plant, and equipment, is a term used in accountancy for assets and property which cannot easily be converted into cash. This can be compared with current assets such as cash or bank accounts, which are described as liquid assets. In most cases, only tangible assets are referred to as fixed.

Chapter 16. Control: Techniques for Enhancing Organizational Effectiveness

a. 33 Strategies of War
c. 1990 Clean Air Act
b. 28-hour day
d. Fixed asset

43. _____ is a company's financial statement that indicates how the revenue is transformed into the net income The purpose of the _____ is to show managers and investors whether the company made or lost money during the period being reported.

The important thing to remember about an _____ is that it represents a period of time.

a. A4e
c. AAAI
b. A Stake in the Outcome
d. Income statement

44. Market _____ is a business, economics or investment term that refers to an asset's ability to be easily converted through an act of buying or selling without causing a significant movement in the price and with minimum loss of value. Money, or cash on hand, is the most liquid asset. An act of exchange of a less liquid asset with a more liquid asset is called liquidation.

a. Liquidity
c. 1990 Clean Air Act
b. 28-hour day
d. 33 Strategies of War

45. _____ is an idea in the field of Organizational studies and management which describes the psychology, attitudes, experiences, beliefs and Values (personal and cultural values) of an organization. It has been defined as 'the specific collection of values and norms that are shared by people and groups in an organization and that control the way they interact with each other and with stakeholders outside the organization.'

This definition continues to explain organizational values also known as 'beliefs and ideas about what kinds of goals members of an organization should pursue and ideas about the appropriate kinds or standards of behavior organizational members should use to achieve these goals. From organizational values develop organizational norms, guidelines or expectations that prescribe appropriate kinds of behavior by employees in particular situations and control the behavior of organizational members towards one another.'

_____ is not the same as corporate culture.

a. Organizational development
c. Organizational effectiveness
b. Organizational culture
d. Union shop

46. An _____ is a practitioner of accountancy, which is the measurement, disclosure or provision of assurance about financial information that helps managers, investors, tax authorities and other decision makers make resource allocation decisions.

The word '_____' is derived from the French 'Compter' which took its origin from the Latin 'Computare'. The word was formerly written in English as 'Accomptant', but in process of time the word, which was always pronounced by dropping the 'p', became gradually changed both in pronunciation and in orthography to its present form.

a. A Stake in the Outcome
b. AAAI
c. Accountant
d. A4e

47. The _____ is given by the United States National Institute of Standards and Technology. Through the actions of the National Productivity Advisory Committee chaired by Jack Grayson, it was established by the Malcolm Baldrige National Quality Improvement Act of 1987 - Public Law 100-107 and named for Malcolm Baldrige, who served as United States Secretary of Commerce during the Reagan administration from 1981 until his 1987 death in a rodeo accident. APQC, , organized the first White House Conference on Productivity, spearheading the creation and design of the _____ in 1987, and jointly administering the award for its first three years.

a. Business Network Transformation
b. Time and attendance
c. Malcolm Baldrige National Quality Award
d. Scenario planning

48. _____ is a business management strategy aimed at embedding awareness of quality in all organizational processes. _____ has been widely used in manufacturing, education, hospitals, call centers, government, and service industries, as well as NASA space and science programs.

As defined by the International Organization for Standardization (ISO):

'_____ is a management approach for an organization, centered on quality, based on the participation of all its members and aiming at long-term success through customer satisfaction, and benefits to all members of the organization and to society.' ISO 8402:1994

One major aim is to reduce variation from every process so that greater consistency of effort is obtained. (Royse, D., Thyer, B., Padgett D., ' Logan T., 2006)

a. 28-hour day
b. 1990 Clean Air Act
c. Quality management
d. Total quality management

49. _____ can be considered to have three main components: quality control, quality assurance and quality improvement. _____ is focused not only on product quality, but also the means to achieve it. _____ therefore uses quality assurance and control of processes as well as products to achieve more consistent quality.

a. 1990 Clean Air Act
b. Quality management
c. Total quality management
d. 28-hour day

50. _____ ('Plan-Do-Check-Act') is an iterative four-step problem-solving process typically used in business process improvement. It is also known as the Deming Cycle, Shewhart cycle, Deming Wheel, or Plan-Do-Study-Act.

_____ was made popular by Dr. W. Edwards Deming, who is considered by many to be the father of modern quality control; however it was always referred to by him as the Shewhart cycle. Later in Deming's career, he modified _____ to Plan, Do, Study, Act (PDSA) so as to better describe his recommendations.

a. Decentralization
b. Management team
c. Management by exception
d. PDCA

Chapter 16. Control: Techniques for Enhancing Organizational Effectiveness

51. A _____ is a group of employees from various functional areas of the organization - research, engineering, marketing, finance. human resources, and operations, for example - who are all focused on a specific objective and are responsible to work as a team to improve coordination and innovation across divisions and resolve mutual problems.
   a. Cross-functional team
   b. Goal-setting theory
   c. Graduate recruitment
   d. Sociotechnical systems

52. The _____ captures an expanded spectrum of values and criteria for measuring organizational success: economic, ecological and social. With the ratification of the United Nations and ICLEI _____ standard for urban and community accounting in early 2007, this became the dominant approach to public sector full cost accounting. Similar UN standards apply to natural capital and human capital measurement to assist in measurements required by _____, e.g. the ecoBudget standard for reporting ecological footprint.
   a. 1990 Clean Air Act
   b. 28-hour day
   c. Triple bottom line
   d. 33 Strategies of War

53. In probability theory, a probability distribution is called _____ if its cumulative distribution function is _____. This is equivalent to saying that for random variables X with the distribution in question, Pr[X = a] = 0 for all real numbers a, i.e.: the probability that X attains the value a is zero, for any number a. If the distribution of X is _____ then X is called a _____ random variable.
   a. Pay Band
   b. Decision tree pruning
   c. Connectionist expert systems
   d. Continuous

54. _____ is a management process whereby delivery (customer valued) processes are constantly evaluated and improved in the light of their efficiency, effectiveness and flexibility.

Some see it as a meta process for most management systems (Business Process Management, Quality Management, Project Management). Deming saw it as part of the 'system' whereby feedback from the process and customer were evaluated against organisational goals.

   a. Sole proprietorship
   b. Critical Success Factor
   c. First-mover advantage
   d. Continuous Improvement Process

55. _____ is a Japanese philosophy that focuses on continuous improvement throughout all aspects of life. When applied to the workplace, _____ activities continually improve all functions of a business, from manufacturing to management and from the CEO to the assembly line workers. By improving standardized activities and processes, _____ aims to eliminate waste .
   a. Sensitivity analysis
   b. Psychological pricing
   c. Cross-docking
   d. Kaizen

56. A _____ is a volunteer group composed of workers (or even students), usually under the leadership of their supervisor (but they can elect a team leader), who are trained to identify, analyse and solve work-related problems and present their solutions to management in order to improve the performance of the organization, and motivate and enrich the work of employees. When matured, true _____s become self-managing, having gained the confidence of management. _____s are an alternative to the dehumanising concept of the Division of Labour, where workers or individuals are treated like robots.

Chapter 16. Control: Techniques for Enhancing Organizational Effectiveness

a. Connectionist expert systems
b. Quality circle
c. Certified in Production and Inventory Management
d. Competency-based job descriptions

57. _____ is a form of communication that typically attempts to persuade potential customers to purchase or to consume more of a particular brand of product or service. 'While now central to the contemporary global economy and the reproduction of global production networks, it is only quite recently that _____ has been more than a marginal influence on patterns of sales and production. The formation of modern _____ was intimately bound up with the emergence of new forms of monopoly capitalism around the end of the 19th and beginning of the 20th century as one element in corporate strategies to create, organize and where possible control markets, especially for mass produced consumer goods.

a. A4e
b. Advertising
c. A Stake in the Outcome
d. AAAI

58. _____ is the process of comparing the cost, cycle time, productivity, or quality of a specific process or method to another that is widely considered to be an industry standard or best practice. Essentially, _____ provides a snapshot of the performance of your business and helps you understand where you are in relation to a particular standard. The result is often a business case for making changes in order to make improvements.

a. Benchmarking
b. Complementors
c. Competitive heterogeneity
d. Cost leadership

59. A _____ is the belief that there is a technique, method, process, activity, incentive or reward that is more effective at delivering a particular outcome than any other technique, method, process, etc. The idea is that with proper processes, checks, and testing, a desired outcome can be delivered with fewer problems and unforeseen complications. _____s can also be defined as the most efficient (least amount of effort) and effective (best results) way of accomplishing a task, based on repeatable procedures that have proven themselves over time for large numbers of people.

a. Design management
b. Hierarchical organization
c. Best practice
d. Fix it twice

60. _____ is the incidence or process of transferring ownership of a business, enterprise, agency or public service from the public sector (government) to the private sector (business.) In a broader sense, _____ refers to transfer of any government function to the private sector including governmental functions like revenue collection and law enforcement.

a. 1990 Clean Air Act
b. Performance reports
c. Privatization
d. 28-hour day

61. The _____, widely known as ISO , is an international-standard-setting body composed of representatives from various national standards organizations. Founded on 23 February 1947, the organization promulgates worldwide proprietary industrial and commercial standards. It is headquartered in Geneva, Switzerland.

a. International Organization for Standardization
b. AAAI
c. A4e
d. A Stake in the Outcome

62. _____ is a business management strategy, initially implemented by Motorola, that today enjoys widespread application in many sectors of industry.

_____ seeks to improve the quality of process outputs by identifying and removing the causes of defects (errors) and variation in manufacturing and business processes. It uses a set of quality management methods, including statistical methods, and creates a special infrastructure of people within the organization ('Black Belts' etc.).

Chapter 16. Control: Techniques for Enhancing Organizational Effectiveness

a. Production line
b. Takt time
c. Theory of constraints
d. Six Sigma

63. _____ is an effective method of monitoring a process through the use of control charts. Control charts enable the use of objective criteria for distinguishing background variation from events of significance based on statistical techniques. Much of its power lies in the ability to monitor both process center and its variation about that center.

a. Single Minute Exchange of Die
b. Quality control
c. Process capability
d. Statistical process control

64. A sample is a subject chosen from a population for investigation. A _____ is one chosen by a method involving an unpredictable component. Random sampling can also refer to taking a number of independent observations from the same probability distribution, without involving any real population.

a. 1990 Clean Air Act
b. 28-hour day
c. 33 Strategies of War
d. Random sample

65. The _____ in statistical process control is a tool used to determine whether a manufacturing or business process is in a state of statistical control or not.

If the chart indicates that the process is currently under control then it can be used with confidence to predict the future performance of the process. If the chart indicates that the process being monitored is not in control, the pattern it reveals can help determine the source of variation to be eliminated to bring the process back into control.

a. Time series analysis
b. Failure rate
c. Simple moving average
d. Control chart

66. A _____ is a common type of chart, that represents an algorithm or process, showing the steps as boxes of various kinds, and their order by connecting these with arrows. _____s are used in analyzing, designing, documenting or managing a process or program in various fields.

The first structured method for documenting process flow, the 'flow process chart', was introduced by Frank Gilbreth to members of ASME in 1921 as the presentation 'Process Charts--First Steps in Finding the One Best Way'.

a. 28-hour day
b. 33 Strategies of War
c. 1990 Clean Air Act
d. Flowchart

67. In statistics, a _____ is a graphical display of tabulated frequencies, shown as bars. It shows what proportion of cases fall into each of several categories: it is a form of data binning. The categories are usually specified as non-overlapping intervals of some variable.

a. Statistics
b. Standard deviation
c. Correlation
d. Histogram

Chapter 16. Control: Techniques for Enhancing Organizational Effectiveness

68. _____ is a statistical technique in decision making that is used for selection of a limited number of tasks that produce significant overall effect. It uses the Pareto principle - the idea that by doing 20% of work you can generate 80% of the advantage of doing the entire job. Or in terms of quality improvement, a large majority of problems (80%) are produced by a few key causes (20%.)
   a. Probability matching
   b. Pareto analysis
   c. Polychoric correlation
   d. Goodness of fit

69. A _____, also known as a run-sequence plot is a graph that displays observed data in a time sequence. Often, the data displayed represent some aspect of the output or performance of a manufacturing or other business process.

   Run sequence plots are an easy way to graphically summarize a univariate data set.
   a. 28-hour day
   b. Run chart
   c. 1990 Clean Air Act
   d. 33 Strategies of War

70. A scatter plot is a type of display using Cartesian coordinates to display values for two variables for a set of data.

   The data is displayed as a collection of points, each having the value of one variable determining the position on the horizontal axis and the value of the other variable determining the position on the vertical axis. A scatter plot is also called a scatter chart, _____ and scatter graph.
   a. 28-hour day
   b. 33 Strategies of War
   c. 1990 Clean Air Act
   d. Scatter diagram

71. An _____ is a situation that will often involve an apparent conflict between moral imperatives, in which to obey one would result in transgressing another. This is also called an ethical paradox since in moral philosophy, paradox plays a central role in ethics debates. For instance, an ethical admonition to 'love thy neighbour as thy self' is not always just in contrast with, but sometimes in contradiction to an armed neighbour actively trying to kill you: if he or she succeeds, you will not be able to love him or her.
   a. A Stake in the Outcome
   b. A4e
   c. AAAI
   d. Ethical dilemma

72. _____ is the temporary suspension or permanent termination of employment of an employee or (more commonly) a group of employees for business reasons, such as the decision that certain positions are no longer necessary or a business slow-down or interruption in work. Originally the term '_____' referred exclusively to a temporary interruption in work, as when factory work cyclically falls off. However, in recent times the term can also refer to the permanent elimination of a position.
   a. Wrongful dismissal
   b. Retirement
   c. Layoff
   d. Termination of employment

73. _____ is a process of planning and controlling the performance or execution of any type of activity, such as:

   - a project (project _____) or
   - a process (process _____, sometimes referred to as the process performance measurement and management system.)

Chapter 16. Control: Techniques for Enhancing Organizational Effectiveness

Organization's senior management is responsible for carrying out its _____.

a. Human Relations Movement
b. Participatory management
c. Work design
d. Management process

74. _____ has been described as the 'process of social influence in which one person can enlist the aid and support of others in the accomplishment of a common task'. A definition more inclusive of followers comes from Alan Keith of Genentech who said '_____ is ultimately about creating a way for people to contribute to making something extraordinary happen.'

_____ is one of the most salient aspects of the organizational context. However, defining _____ has been challenging.

a. 1990 Clean Air Act
b. Leadership
c. 28-hour day
d. Situational leadership

ANSWER KEY

Chapter 1
1. a	2. d	3. b	4. d	5. b	6. a	7. a	8. c	9. c	10. d
11. d	12. a	13. d	14. d	15. d	16. b	17. d	18. d	19. b	20. d
21. b	22. a	23. c	24. c	25. a	26. d	27. c	28. d	29. b	30. d
31. a	32. d	33. c	34. b	35. a	36. a	37. b	38. a	39. a	40. d
41. c	42. a	43. b	44. c	45. d	46. a	47. d			

Chapter 2
1. d	2. d	3. c	4. d	5. b	6. a	7. b	8. d	9. b	10. d
11. d	12. b	13. b	14. d	15. d	16. a	17. d	18. d	19. c	20. d
21. d	22. d	23. d	24. b	25. b	26. d	27. a	28. b	29. d	30. c
31. d	32. b	33. d	34. a	35. d	36. c	37. a	38. d	39. b	40. d
41. d	42. d	43. a	44. a	45. c					

Chapter 3
1. d	2. b	3. d	4. d	5. a	6. b	7. d	8. b	9. d	10. d
11. d	12. d	13. d	14. b	15. d	16. c	17. c	18. d	19. b	20. d
21. d	22. d	23. d	24. d	25. d	26. b	27. c	28. b	29. c	30. d
31. a	32. a	33. b	34. a	35. d	36. a	37. d	38. a	39. a	40. a
41. b	42. b	43. a	44. d	45. d	46. d	47. b	48. a	49. d	50. b
51. a	52. d	53. d	54. d	55. c	56. c				

Chapter 4
1. d	2. d	3. d	4. c	5. b	6. d	7. a	8. b	9. d	10. d
11. b	12. d	13. d	14. a	15. d	16. c	17. d	18. b	19. c	20. c
21. d	22. d	23. d	24. a	25. d	26. d	27. c	28. c	29. a	30. d
31. d	32. a	33. d	34. a	35. d	36. d	37. c	38. d	39. b	40. a
41. d	42. a	43. a	44. d	45. d	46. a	47. c	48. d		

Chapter 5
1. b	2. a	3. b	4. a	5. d	6. d	7. a	8. d	9. b	10. d
11. d	12. d	13. d	14. d	15. b	16. d	17. a	18. c	19. a	20. d
21. d	22. d	23. d	24. d	25. c	26. d	27. d			

Chapter 6
1. d	2. d	3. b	4. d	5. a	6. c	7. b	8. d	9. b	10. a
11. d	12. d	13. d	14. b	15. a	16. c	17. d	18. d	19. d	20. c
21. d	22. c	23. a	24. b	25. d	26. c	27. d	28. d	29. a	30. c
31. a	32. d	33. d	34. a	35. b	36. d	37. d	38. d	39. d	40. d
41. d	42. a	43. c	44. d						

Chapter 7
1. c	2. a	3. c	4. d	5. d	6. b	7. d	8. d	9. b	10. a
11. c	12. a	13. b	14. c	15. d	16. d	17. a	18. d	19. b	20. a
21. d	22. d	23. d	24. a	25. d	26. d	27. d	28. d	29. b	30. d
31. b	32. a	33. b	34. d						

ANSWER KEY

Chapter 8
1. d   2. d   3. d   4. b   5. d   6. d   7. a   8. b   9. b   10. d
11. c   12. d   13. d   14. a   15. b   16. a   17. c   18. d   19. b   20. a
21. b   22. d   23. d   24. c   25. a   26. d   27. d   28. a   29. c   30. b
31. b

Chapter 9
1. d   2. d   3. a   4. d   5. d   6. b   7. d   8. c   9. d   10. b
11. d   12. d   13. c   14. d   15. a   16. a   17. c   18. b   19. d   20. d
21. d   22. d   23. d   24. d   25. d   26. d   27. a   28. d   29. d   30. d
31. d   32. b   33. d   34. d   35. d   36. d   37. d   38. b   39. c   40. c
41. b   42. b   43. d   44. d   45. a   46. b   47. d   48. a   49. d   50. d
51. b   52. c   53. d   54. a   55. c   56. b   57. d

Chapter 10
1. d   2. d   3. d   4. b   5. d   6. d   7. d   8. d   9. d   10. d
11. d   12. b   13. d   14. d   15. d   16. d   17. d   18. d   19. d   20. b
21. d   22. c   23. d   24. b   25. d   26. c   27. d   28. b   29. c   30. c
31. d   32. d

Chapter 11
1. b   2. d   3. d   4. d   5. d   6. a   7. c   8. d   9. d   10. d
11. b   12. d   13. d   14. d   15. a   16. d   17. d   18. d   19. a   20. b
21. c   22. d   23. c   24. d   25. c   26. d   27. b   28. d   29. a   30. d
31. c   32. a   33. c   34. a

Chapter 12
1. b   2. d   3. b   4. c   5. d   6. a   7. d   8. d   9. d   10. a
11. d   12. d   13. a   14. d   15. b   16. c   17. d   18. b   19. d   20. b
21. c   22. d   23. b   24. a   25. a   26. a   27. a   28. a   29. d   30. c
31. d   32. a   33. d   34. d   35. d   36. d   37. d   38. a   39. c   40. d
41. c   42. b

Chapter 13
1. d   2. a   3. c   4. d   5. d   6. b   7. d   8. c   9. c   10. b
11. d   12. d   13. b   14. d   15. d   16. d   17. d   18. c   19. d   20. a
21. d   22. b   23. d   24. b   25. d   26. d

Chapter 14
1. c   2. c   3. d   4. d   5. d   6. d   7. c   8. a   9. a   10. a
11. d   12. d   13. d   14. c   15. d   16. d   17. a   18. a   19. c   20. d
21. c   22. d   23. d

Chapter 15
1. d	2. d	3. d	4. d	5. d	6. c	7. c	8. a	9. d	10. d
11. d	12. c	13. b	14. b	15. a	16. b	17. d			

Chapter 16
1. b	2. d	3. c	4. d	5. a	6. b	7. d	8. d	9. d	10. d
11. d	12. d	13. c	14. d	15. a	16. b	17. d	18. d	19. d	20. d
21. d	22. d	23. d	24. b	25. d	26. a	27. d	28. d	29. b	30. d
31. c	32. a	33. a	34. b	35. d	36. a	37. d	38. d	39. b	40. b
41. a	42. d	43. d	44. a	45. b	46. c	47. c	48. d	49. b	50. d
51. a	52. c	53. d	54. d	55. d	56. b	57. b	58. a	59. c	60. c
61. a	62. d	63. d	64. d	65. d	66. d	67. d	68. b	69. b	70. d
71. d	72. c	73. d	74. b						